Renzo Piano Centre Kanak

Werner Blaser

Renzo Piano   Centre Kanak

Kulturzentrum der Kanak
Cultural Center of the Kanak People

Birkhäuser – Publishers for Architecture
Basel · Boston · Berlin

This publication was kindly supported by:

Diese Publikation wurde freundlicherweise unterstützt von:

Regent Beleuchtungskörper AG, Basel, www.regent.ch

Translations:

German into English: Katja Steiner, Bruce Almberg, Ehingen

French into German: Barbara Heber-Schärer, Berlin

French into English: Sarah Parsons, Paris

A CIP catalogue record for this book is available from the Library of Congress, Washington D.C., USA.

Deutsche Bibliothek Cataloging-in-Publication Data

[Renzo Piano - Centre Kanak] Renzo Piano - Centre Kanak, Kulturzentrum der Kanak,

Cultural Center of the Kanak People / Werner Blaser. [Transl.: German into Engl.: Katja Steiner…].

- Basel ; Boston ; Berlin : Birkhäuser, 2001

ISBN 3-7643-6540-4

© 2001 Birkhäuser – Publishers for Architecture, P.O. Box 133, CH-4010 Basel, Switzerland.
    Member of the BertelsmannSpringer Publishing Group.

Layout: Werner Blaser, Basel

Litho and typography: Photolitho Sturm AG, Muttenz

Printed on acid-free paper produced of chlorine-free pulp. TCF ∞

Printed in Germany

ISBN 3-7643-6540-4

9 8 7 6 5 4 3 2 1   http://www.birkhauser.ch

Inhaltsverzeichnis

Contents

Geleitwort

Das vorliegende Buch will in Bild und Text ein außergewöhnliches Werk des Architekten Renzo Piano vorstellen. Außergewöhnlich war schon die Aufgabe, der sich der europäische Architekt vor Ort, also fast bei den Antipoden, mit Herz und Geist gestellt hat, um sie mit Bravour zu lösen. Die Aufgabe lautete, dem neu zu gründenden «Centre culturel Jean-Marie Tjibaou» in Nouméa eine bauliche Gestalt zu geben, die in Form und Funktion Wertschätzung für die Kultur der Kanak – das heißt der einheimischen Bevölkerung von Neukaledonien und den Loyalty-Inseln – zum Ausdruck bringen sollte. Vom Architekten wurde das fast Unmögliche erwartet, sollte sein Werk, anzusiedeln am Rand der stark europäisch geprägten Stadt Nouméa, doch zugleich offen für zukünftige schöpferische Leistungen der Bevölkerungsgruppen Neukaledoniens und der Loyalty-Inseln sein und Respekt bezeugen vor den einheimischen kulturellen Überlieferungen.

Die Qualität der Lösung von Renzo Piano erweist sich darin, daß das vollendete Werk dem Besucher des Kulturzentrums in der Tat Lebensart und Denkweise der Kanak-Bevölkerung ohne Zwang näherbringt, ihm Lesarten vorschlägt, die zu bewältigen sind. Die unter der Ägide der «Agence de Développement de la Culture Kanak» (A.D.C.K.) vorgenommene Einrichtung des Zentrums zielt darauf, den Besucher mit der Vielfalt der einheimischen kulturellen Überlieferungen vertraut zu machen, ohne ihn mit Fakten zu überfüttern. Die kolonialen Traumata werden dabei angesprochen. Zugleich gelingt es, zeitgenössische künstlerische Ausdrucksformen bewußt als Weg des Kommunizierens zwischen Individuen, Gruppen und Bevölkerungsteilen einzusetzen.

Nicht weniger als 28 verschiedene Sprachen, nicht Dialekte, wurden und werden zum größten Teil noch gesprochen auf dem Territorium dieser südlichsten Inseln von Melanesien. Alle Sprachen gehören zur austronesischen Sprachfamilie; sie reichen in ihren Wurzeln vermutlich zurück bis zu den ersten Einwanderern, die vor rund 3000 oder mehr Jahren die Hauptinsel Neukaledonien übers Meer erreicht haben. Wie im Südpazifik allgemein üblich, sind auch hier immer wieder einige weitergezogen, während andere – die einheiratenden Frauen etwa, die Tauschbeziehungen zwischen Klanverbänden folgten, oder aber einzelne unternehmungslustige Häuptlinge mit Gefolgsleuten – von außen dazustießen.

Die genuine Leistung von Renzo Piano besteht darin, in der Auseinandersetzung mit den Zeugen und Zeugnissen dieser Kultur, mit den heutigen Menschen also und den von ihren Vorfahren geschaffenen Ausdrucksformen, dem Wesentlichen eine neue architektonische Form verliehen zu haben.

Der französische Anthropologe Alban Bensa und die Mitarbeiter der Entwicklungsagentur A.D.C.K. mögen dem Architekten den Zugang zum politischen und intellektuellen Werk von Jean-Marie Tjibaou (1936–1989) erleichtert und ihm Erkenntnisse der Ethnologie über die Gesellschaft der Kanak aufbereitet haben; Bensa berichtet darüber in seinem neuesten Buch. Als Architekt und damit auch als Autor seines architektonischen Werkes mußte sich Piano allerdings selbst auf die Auseinandersetzung einlassen, um eine tragfähige Antwort zu finden. Dabei kam ihm Jean-Marie Tjibaous Leitgedanke entgegen. Dieser hatte die Kanak-Bevölkerung wiederholt zur Einsicht ermuntert, ihre Identität liege vor ihr, sie sei aus

Preface

This book hopes to present an unusual work of the architect Renzo Piano through the use of images and text. The task that the European architect had set for himself with heart and spirit on site – almost at the Antipodes – which he solved in a brilliant way, was already unusual enough as a challenge. The task was to provide the newly founded Centre Culturel Jean-Marie Tjibaou in Nouméa with an architectural gestalt that would express an appreciation for the culture of the Kanak – the native population of New Caledonia and the Loyalty Islands – in both form and function. The almost impossible was expected from the architect: his work, which was to be located at the periphery of the city of Nouméa, a city with a strong European influence, was to be open for future creative achievements of the population groups of New Caledonia and the Loyality Islands and, at the same time, would pay respect to the local cultural traditions.

The quality of Renzo Piano's solution reveals itself in the fact that, without force, the completed oeuvre indeed brings the lifestyle and way of thinking of the Kanak population closer to the visitors of the cultural center, while also suggesting to them versions that need to be dealt with. The establishment of the center carried out under the auspices of the "Agence de Dévelopement de la Culture Kanak" (A.D.C.K.) aims at familiarizing visitors with the versatility of the local cultural traditions without overloading them with facts. The colonial traumas are addressed. At the same time, contemporary artistic forms of expressions are successfully and consciously used as ways of communicating between individuals, groups and segments of the population.

No less than 28 different languages, not dialects, were and are for the most part still spoken on the territory of these most southern islands of Melanesia. All of the languages are part of the Austronesian language family; their roots probably extend back to the first immigrants who crossed the ocean to reach the main island of New Caledonia about 3000 or more years ago. As is generally customary in the South Pacific, some always moved on, while others – generally women marrying into clans following the links of exchange relationships or individual enterprising chiefs with their followers – joined from the outside. The genuine achievement of Renzo Piano was to provide the essential with a new architectural gestalt in the confrontation with the witnesses of this culture, today's inhabitants and the forms of expression created by their ancestors.

The French anthropologist Alban Bensa and the staff of the development agency A.D.C.K. may have facilitated access to the political and intellectual oeuvre of Jean-Marie Tjibaou (1936–1989) for the architect and offered him insights about the society of the Kanak. Bensa reports about this in his latest book. However, as an architect and thus the author of his architectural oeuvre, Renzo Piano had to get into the confrontation in order to find a sound answer. Jean-Marie Tjibaou's central theme came towards him. He had repeatedly encouraged the Kanak population to see that its culture is right before their eyes, that it can be reestablished out of today's life and experience and even conquered. The opposite direction – that is, wanting to copy their own identity from tradition – would in Tjibaou's opinion have had no

dem heutigen Leben und Erleben heraus neu zu bestimmen, ja zu erobern. Ohne Aussicht auf Gelingen wäre dagegen der bislang vertraute Weg in die entgegengesetzte Richtung, so Tjibaous Überzeugung, nämlich die eigene Identität aus der Tradition einfach herüberkopieren zu wollen. Tjibaou hat damit einen wichtigen, über die eklektizistische Postmoderne hinausweisenden Schritt getan. Wohl ist das Wissen um den Inhalt der einzelnen Traditionen wertvoll und wichtig, aber: Die Traditionen vermögen in der heutigen, vom Bewußtwerden ihrer eigenen Komplexität herausgeforderten Welt nicht mehr allein unser zukünftiges Sein zu bestimmen.

Renzo Pianos Rundbauten und ihre Anordnung in Weilern oder «Villages» entlang einer Achse setzen diese Vision Jean-Marie Tjibaous in klarer, kongenialer Form in die gebaute Realität um. Der Bau und seine von Piano lieber mit einem präzisen und feinen Spatel als mit der Baggerschaufel gestaltete Umgebung schaffen so einen Rahmen für den stets weiterlaufenden, also offenen Schöpfungsprozeß, in dem die Identität der Kanak neu zu bestimmen ist. Apropos Einpassung in die Umgebung: Piano regte an, die Geländenase an der Lagune mit einem Initiationspfad zu erschließen und so eine direkte Verbindung zwischen Bau und Landschaft einerseits und zwischen Gegenwart und Tradition anderseits zu schaffen. Der Gang entlang diesem «Chemin Kanak» wird in der Tat für viele Besucher zum bestimmenden Erlebnis.

10 Das gebaute Werk, dessen Achse sich über 220 m erstreckt, kündet somit von der Ambition der Geehrten wie von der Leistungskraft seines Entwerfers. Aufgabe und Lösung stehen, so können wir heute feststellen, im Gleichklang. Sie verknüpfen in geglückter Form die gedankliche Durchdringung mit der Ausdruckskraft des Bauwerks: handfest, zugleich im Boden verwurzelt wie die Taroknollen in der Pflanzung am «Chemin Kanak» und doch schwebend, nach oben weisend wie die Araukarien neben den Rundbauten und zugleich fortstrebend wie die alten Doppelkanus mit ihren geschwellten Segeln, dabei aus dem Blickpunkt des Meisters sowohl den Ausgangspunkt als auch das Ziel der Wanderfahrt im Auge behaltend.

Zu Beginn der Bauperiode, als der angestrebte Gleichklang zwischen Auftrag und Funktion gefährdet schien, wurden auswärtige Fachpersonen aus dem Bereich des Süd-Pazifiks und Europas ausgewählt und um ihren Kommentar wie auch um ihre Vorschläge gebeten. Der Meinungsaustausch dieses sogenannten «Comité de pilotage» stand von 1994 bis 1998 unter der Leitung von Marie-Claude Tjibaou. Es galt, eine gemeinsame Vision für die möglichen Inhalte und Arbeitsweisen des Zentrums zu entwickeln. Als am Rande Beteiligter darf man heute feststellen, in welch glücklicher Weise die Vision des Architekten sich erfüllt hat und wie gut der Bau den Bedürfnissen sowohl der Betreiber wie auch der Benutzer dient.

Natürlich sind nicht für alle Beteiligten die Erwartungen gleichermaßen in Erfüllung gegangen. Der Bericht des Direktors der A.D.C.K. für kulturelle Aufgaben und Leiter des Zentrums, Emmanuel Kasarhérou, belegt, daß das Zentrum für alle Besucher, die den Weg nicht scheuen, erfolgreich funktioniert. Neuer-

chance of being successful. With this, Tjibaou has taken an important step that goes beyond eclectic post-modernism. The knowledge of the content of the individual traditions is valuable and important; however, in today's world traditions alone are not capable of determining our future existence, which is challenged by the awareness of its own complexity. Renzo Piano's round buildings and their arrangement in "villages" along an axis realize this vision of Jean-Marie Tjibaou in a clear and congenial form. The building and its environment, designed by Piano rather with a precise and fine spatula instead of the backhoe, thus create a framework for the always continuing, i.e., open, creative process in which the identity of the Kanak can be reestablished. As an appropriate integration into the environment, Piano suggested developing the promontory at the lagoon with an initiation path thus establishing a direct connection between the building and landscape on one hand, and between the present and tradition on the other hand. The walk along this Chemin Kanak indeed becomes a decisive experience.

The constructed oeuvre, whose axis expands over 220 meters, thus tells about the ambition of those honored and of the power of achievement of its designer. As we can see today, the task and the solution are in harmony. They link the intellectual permeation with the expression of the building in a successful way: down-to-earth, at the same time rooted in the ground like the Taro bulb and yet floating, striving upwards like the Araucaria planted along Chemin Kanak, moving away like the double canoes with their swelling sails and yet keeping an eye from the point of view of the master on the starting point and the destination of the voyage.

As at the beginning of the construction period the aim for harmony between instruction and function seemed endangered, foreign experts from all over the South Pacific and Europe were asked for their comments and input. The exchange of views of this so-called "Comité de pilotage" was influenced by the leadership of Marie-Claude Tjibaou from 1994 to 1998. The committee's aim was to develop a common vision regarding the possible contents and methods of working concerning the center. As a participant I note with great satisfaction that the vision of the architect has become true and the building serves the needs of both the operators and users in a fortunate way.

Of course, not all participants' expectations have been equally fulfilled. The report of Emmanuel Kasarhérou, director of the center and of the cultural programme of the A.D.C.K., proves that the center functions with great success for all the visitors who don't mind the distance. Recently, the connection to the city of Nouméa, which is decisive for the continued prospering of the center, could be strikingly improved through a regularly functioning public bus connection. However, it will probably still take years before the visits by the Kanak youths to the peripherally located peninsula Tina with its médiathèque, library and special exhibitions will again reach the intensity that existed during the years of the provisional center located in the inner city of Nouméa. This aspect is of course beyond the responsibility of the architect as Jean-Marie Tjibaou himself chose the site.

On 4 May 1998, speaking to many guests of honor from all Pacific states, the French Prime Minister

dings konnte die für das weitere Gedeihen entscheidende Anbindung an die Stadt Nouméa durch eine regelmäßig verkehrende öffentliche Buslinie markant verbessert werden. Allerdings wird es wohl noch Jahre dauern, bis auf der peripher gelegenen Halbinsel Tina für die Kanak-Jugend der Besuch des Zentrums mit seiner Mediathek, seiner Bibliothek und den Sonderausstellungen wieder die Intensität der Jahre des Provisoriums in der Innenstadt von Nouméa erreichen wird. Dieser Aspekt fällt freilich nicht in die Verantwortung des Architekten. Jean-Marie Tjibaou selbst hatte den Ort gewählt.

Besser, als einführende Worte von Außenstehenden es vermögen, hat Frau Marie-Claude Tjibaou, Präsidentin der A.D.C.K., am 4. Mai 1998 vor vielen Ehrengästen aus allen Pazifik-Staaten, vor dem französischen Ministerpräsidenten Lionel Jospin und den zuständigen Ressortministern den Punkt beschrieben und erläutert, an dem Vision und Vermächtnis von Jean-Marie Tjibaou erstmals für sein Volk und dessen Nachbarn sichtbare Gestalt angenommen haben. Der Text ist herzlich, direkt und frei von Politikerfloskeln und belegt damit eindrücklich, in welchem Maße der Architekt mit seiner ebenso von Herzen kommenden, direkt ansprechenden und schnörkellosen Leistung zum stärksten Übermittler dieser zukunftsgerichteten Vision geworden ist.

12 Sommer 2001
Christian Kaufmann, Basel

Lionel Jospin and the responsible ministers, and using better introductory words than those an outsider could express, Ms. Marie-Claude Tjibaou, President of the A.D.C.K. described and explained the point at which the vision and legacy of Jean-Marie Tjibaou for the first time took a visible shape for his people and their neighbors. The text is heartfelt, direct and free of political rhetoric and thus impressively proves the degree to which the architect, with his also heartfelt, directly appealing and no-frills achievement, has become the strongest communicator of this future-oriented vision.

Summer 2001
Christian Kaufmann, Basel

Das Kulturzentrum in Nouméa zur Pflege der Kanak-Kultur von Renzo Piano stellt ein vollendetes Meisterwerk und ein zutiefst beeindruckendes, erdgebundenes Beispiel einer neuen Interpretation der Moderne dar. Es vereint die alten und neuen Stilmittel aufs Genialste, ein architektonisch-technologisches Werk, das wie kaum ein anderes zu berühren vermag. Es ist eine Umsetzung des traditionellen örtlichen Rundhauses der Einheimischen. Um so erstaunlicher ist es, daß das Ergebnis wie ein Original dasteht, als einheitliches, geschlossenes Ganzes. Zehn Hütten-Pavillons in heutiger Holztechnologie, nebeneinander aufgereiht, deren Transparenz und Dichte zugleich Leichtigkeit und Schwere, hell und dunkel erzeugen.

Renzo Piano realisierte im Pazifik auf Neukaledonien die Idee vom Gesamtkunstwerk, indem von ein und derselben Hand das Gebäude und alle Details konzipiert wurden. Sein obsessives Credo an das Konstrukt erwies sich als genial, indem er darin seine Ideen der Ingenieurbaukunst vereinigte. Geschickt setzt er das Widerspiel des räumlichen Verengens und Öffnens bei den Pavillons ein, um den Gebäuden so Atem einzuhauchen. Durch die gesteigerte Dynamik der bewegten Holzkonstruktion wird die Architektur vor gänzlich neue Herausforderungen gestellt. Diese impulsive Gestalt wurde aus einem virtuosen Ineinandergreifen und Durchdringen von Raumeinheiten entwickelt. Das enthemmte Streben nach visuellen Effekten ist ganz auf die sinnliche Präsentation der Gestalt abgestimmt.

14 Die Regie von Renzo Piano im Umgang mit den Mega-Strukturen aus widerstandsfähigem Irokoholz zeigt die klare Geometrie im lebendigen Kontrast zur organischen Natur. Er war mutig genug, sich dem schwierigen Erbe des heimischen Rundhauses zu stellen und in der neugeschaffenen Gestalt die Tradition erkennbar zu machen. Die Vorliebe für einfache, langlebige Materialien, gepaart mit einer eigentlichen Besessenheit in der Detailgestaltung, zeigt sich vornehmlich an der laminierten Holzkonstruktion. Alltagstauglich ist das Gebäude, kühn, klar und mit Präzision konstruiert.

Das Schöne verbindet das Sinnliche mit dem Geistigen

Ein Meister wie Renzo Piano macht auf sympathische Weise aus Nöten Tugenden. Darum ist er zur Architektur geboren. So sieht er etwa das Primat der Konstruktion, die wir hier «Holz-tech» nennen. Er gibt seiner räumlichen Inszenierung im Kulturzentrum der Kanak jene Gestalt, nach der wir so dringend trachten. Er läßt keinen Zweifel daran, daß mittels Sensibilität und Durchhaltevermögen ein Architekturereignis stattfinden kann.

Nach fünfzigjähriger Berufserfahrung darf ich sagen, daß eine meiner Hauptverantwortungen im Leben darin besteht, Architektur begreifbar zu machen. Nur eine bewußt gemachte Haltung kann Wissen und Bildung befördern. Das beeindruckende Schaffen in Neukaledonien soll die Neugier wecken für eine Persönlichkeit, die das Bauschaffen entscheidend prägt und auf aktuelle Fragen Antworten bereithält. Denn

Centre Kanak 1993–1998

The cultural center in Nouméa for the preservation of the Kanak culture by Renzo Paino represents a perfected masterpiece and a deeply impressive, earth-bound example of a new interpretation of modernism. It unites the old and new stylistic means in a most ingenious way, an architectural technological oeuvre that is capable of touching us like hardly any other. It is a realization of the traditional local roundhouse of the natives. Therefore – with ten hut pavilions in contemporary wood technology, lined up side by side, whose transparency and density simultaneously create lightness and weight, light and dark – it is even more amazing that the result looks like an original, unified, homogeneous whole.

Renzo Piano realized the idea of the holistic work of art in the Pacific in New Caledonia by conceiving the building and all details as one. His obsessive doctrine, oriented toward the construct, proved to be ingenious in the way it fuses his ideas of engineered architecture. He cleverly uses the counter effect of the spatial narrowing and opening up of the pavilions in order to breathe life into the buildings. The enhanced dynamics of the moved wood construction confronts architecture with entirely new challenges. This impulsive gestalt was developed out of a virtuous overlapping and permeation of spatial units. The uninhibited aspiration for visual effects is completely tuned to the sensual presentation of the gestalt.

The direction Renzo Piano took in constructing the megastructures out of highly durable Iroko wood, shows the clear geometry in a lively contrast with nature. He was courageous enough to face the burden of the heritage of the local roundhouse and to make the tradition visible in the newly created gestalt. The preference for simple, durable materials paired with an obsession with the design of the details is mainly expressed in the laminated wood construction. The building is constructed boldly, clearly and with precision, and is suitable for everyday use.

The Beautiful Combines the Sensual with the Spiritual

A master like Renzo Piano turns necessities into virtues in a sympathetic way. In this way, he seems born to create architecture. For example, he sees not only the primal nature of the construction that we call "wood-tech", but he also provides his spatial production in the cultural center of the Kanak with the gestalt that we so urgently desire, leaving no doubt that, through the means of sensitivity and stamina, an architectural event can take place.

After fifty years of professional experience, I dare say that one of my main responsibilities in life is to make architecture understandable. Only an attitude that is made conscious can promote knowledge and education. The impressive work in New Caledonia should awaken the curiosity to a personality who decisively influences architecture and offers answers to topical questions, because only those who know the profession become free enough to allow the present to enter. At the same time, this also implies a remembrance of roots, as is the case with Renzo Piano in the Building Workshop. Listening within one-

nur wer das Metier kennt, wird frei für die Gegenwart. Gleichzeitig beinhaltet dies auch eine Rückbesinnung auf die Wurzeln, wie bei Renzo Piano im Building Workshop. Dabei wird das In-sich-Hineinhorchen in der Sammlung von Ideen eine Art Selbstvergessenheit. So verbindet das Verlangen nach dem Schönen das Sinnliche mit dem Geistigen. Es zeigt sich eine berufliche Ausrichtung im Bemühen um eine klare Ordnung, im Dialog als Fundament verantwortlicher Lösungen, im Ablehnen isolierten Schwärmertums, in nachvollziehbarer Klarheit.

In der Wahrheit gestalten

Gute Architektur ist immer die Bemühung des einzelnen, das Schöne zu verwirklichen. In dieser Klarheit wachsen zu wollen ist die Bedingung aller gehaltvollen Baukunst. Karl Jaspers: «Die Wahrheit ist unendlich, das Falsche endlos. Wahrheit baut auf, Falschheit zerstört sich selber.» Es ist immer wieder erstaunlich, mit welcher Selbstverständlichkeit außerordentliche Architektur entsteht. Es sind in der Tat Temperamente, die durch Energie, geistige Präsenz und Instinkt für reale Kräfte gültige Ideen in Realität umsetzen können. Weiter gehört ins Anforderungsprofil des Meisterarchitekten, die Offenheit im Konstruktiven zu bewahren, das Einfache herauszuheben, es zu konzentrieren, um es in seinem Inneren zu erhellen.

Das Gegenwärtige zu leben ist der wesentliche Sinn unserer Arbeit. Denn dem Kommenden dienen wir nur, wenn wir in der Tat Gegenwärtiges verwirklichen. Auf der Suche nach der geistigen Ordnung in der Architektur werden überlieferte Werte bedeutsam, hier etwa die der Traditionen der Kanak. Aus der Bewährung müßte Verwandlung entstehen. Dennoch bleibt das Bild der heutigen Architektur zwiespältig, vielleicht trostloser und chancenreicher als je zuvor.

Bauen als Innerlichkeit

Die reine «Holz-tech»-Konstruktion und der logische Aufbau ihres Gesamtsystems bilden in ihrer Strenge eine höchst eindrückliche Struktur. Eine solche Systematisierung leitet auch die Natur. Wenn wir diesem Ingenieur folgen, entdecken wir die Vollkommenheit des konstruktiven Ausdrucks in natürlicher Weise. Eine eindeutige, kompromißlose Stärke im strukturellen Bereich erfüllt das Bauwerk.
Im Material Holz ist jene Textur geschaffen, die alles umfaßt und deren Allseitigkeit den eigentlichen Wert eines Bauwerks ausmacht. In der Raumdurchdringung von innen nach außen finden sich Elemente, die mehr erahnt als erkannt werden können und Aufschlüsse über den Sinn des Raumes bieten. In all diesen Schichten der Holzlamellen-Verkleidung schimmert die Proportion durch und lebt der Raum fort.

self to the collection of ideas transforms one into a kind of being lost in thought. The desire for the beautiful thus combines the sensual with the spiritual. A professional approach presents itself in various ways: in the effort to achieve a clear structure, in dialog as the foundation of responsible solutions, in rejecting isolated enthusiasm, and in an understandable clarity.

Designing in Truth

Good architecture is always a result of an effort by the individual to realize the beautiful. The desire to grow within this clarity is the condition for all profound architecture. Karl Jaspers said, "The truth is infinite, the false is endless. Truth builds up, falseness destroys itself". It is always astonishing with what kind of self-evidence exceptional architecture is created. Indeed, it is temperaments that can realize valid ideas through vitality, mental presence and an instinct for real forces. Another aspect of the profile requirement for the master architect is to preserve the openness in the constructive, to emphasize the simple, and to concentrate it in order to enlighten its inner being.

Living within the present is the essential sense of our work. Because we only serve what's to come if we indeed realize the present. In the search for the spiritual order in architecture, traditional values become important – here, for example, with the understanding of the tradition of the Kanak. Transformation would have to emerge from the already proven. Still, the picture of today's architecture remains conflicting, perhaps more hopeless, while filled with more opportunities than ever before.

Building as an Inwardness

The pure "wood-tech" construction and the logical structure of its overall system form, in their strictness, a highly impressive structure. Such a systematization also guides nature. If we follow this engineer we'll discover the perfection of the constructive expression in a natural way. An unmistakable uncompromising strength in the structural realm fills the building. Wood, whose universal characteristics constitute the real value of a building, creates the texture that comprises everything. In the spatial permeation from inside to outside, elements can be found that can be sensed more than recognized and offer information about the sense of the space. The proportion shimmers through all these layers of the wooden lamellar cladding, adding life to the room. Modulation and harmony result, comparable with the recording of a musical composition. Everything thus falls into order.

The inwardness of Renzo Piano's architecture can be read in the well-proven and always returning principles found throughout the buildings within the total complex at Nouméa: the primacy of construction,

Es entstehen Modulation und Harmonie, vergleichbar mit dem Aufnehmen einer musikalischen Komposition. Dadurch bekommt alles eine Ordnung.

Die Innerlichkeit der Architektur ist bei Renzo Piano in den Gebäuden der Gesamtanlage in Nouméa an den schon bewährten, immer wiederkehrenden Prinzipien ablesbar: Primat der Konstruktion, Werte der Materialien, Raumdurchdringung, Harmonie der Proportion, Auseinandersetzung mit Kunstwerken. Bei der gegenseitigen Beeinflussung dieser fünf Prinzipien gilt es, Gültiges daraus zu entnehmen und die Sinngehalte herauszudestillieren. Diese grundlegenden Werte führen zur Innerlichkeit. In diesem Geiste spiegelt sich das Klare und Schlichte. Denn im Aufgreifen des natürlich Gegebenen und in der Reduktion zum Einfachen liegt das Wesen der Architektur. Einen treffenden Kommentar zu den Gedankengängen, was Schlichtheit sein kann, finden wir schon bei Hellmut Wilhelms Buch über I Ging, «Die Wandlung»: «Das Gute, das im Einfachen und Leichten liegt, setzt es der höchsten Seinsart gleich.» An anderer Stelle heißt es: «Das Reine und Schlichte ist das höchste Gut.» Der allumfassende Begriff des Schlichten und Einfachen eröffnet uns den unmittelbaren Bezug in die Gegenwart.

Im Spiel der Kreativität

Wir erleben mit Sorge jene wachsende kulturelle Gleichförmigkeit, die sich in der Trivialarchitektur landauf landab ausdrückt – überall ein Bauen ohne Gestalt. Die Gegenläufigkeit der architektonischen Entwicklungstendenzen entspricht unserer technischen Welt mit mehr Transparenz. Es bedarf des Glaubens an die Nützlichkeit – auch Wirklichkeit – des moralischen Fortschritts hin zur wahren Architektur. Eine Baukunst, die sich zwischen Behauptung der alten, bewährten Werte und Erkundung des Neuen im Geist der Zeit genuin ausdrückt, wie wir dies bei Renzo Piano immer wieder erfahren. Die Aufgabe ist klar. Wir sollten ein Bauwerk stärker öffnen und mit gestalterischer Integration durchdringen: Eine zeitgenössische Architektur von zeitloser Schönheit und Selbstverständlichkeit.

Architektur nur im Zusammenhang mit Originalität zu sehen kann falsch sein. Es geht nicht um die «Gestalt-Erfindung», sondern um die «Gestalt-Findung»: Man findet das Wahre und Unabhängige. Oder wie es Mies van der Rohe ausdrückte: «Ich will die Form und keine Formspielerei.» Wenn man diesen Satz ernst nimmt, wird man die Architektur dort sehen, wo sie wirklich reine Gestalt sein will.

Bei Renzo Piano ist das eigene Weltbild immer mit der allgemeinen Kreativität verbunden: mit dem Ursprung der Natur und dem Natürlichen. Der kreative Gedanke zeigt sich in der «göttlichen Eingebung», auch in der spontanen Entscheidung oder im intuitiven Bewußtsein. Bei der spielerischen Tätigkeit ist das Kreative nahe, ja im Spiel liegt der Ursprung der Kreativität. Dazu braucht es die eigene Motivation und die freie Zielsetzung sowie die Verfügbarkeit zum freien Nachdenken.

the values of the materials, spatial permeations, harmony of proportion, confrontation with works of art. The point of the mutual interaction of these five principles is to take what is valid from them and to distil the meaningful content. These fundamental values lead to inwardness. In this spirit, the clear and simple is reflected because the essence of architecture lies in taking up the naturally given and reducing them towards simplicity. We can already find a fitting comment regarding the ideas about what simplicity can be from Hellmut Wilhelm: I Ging, Die Wandlung: "The good that lies in the simple and easy is equivalent to the highest form of being". In a different place, he says, "The pure and simple is the highest good". The all-embracing concept of the simple and easy opens up immediate access to the present for us.

Creative Play

We are experiencing with great concern that a growing cultural uniformity is being expressed throughout the country in trivial architecture – building without gestalt is taking place everywhere. The countermovement of architectural developmental tendencies is complying with our technological world with greater transparency, requiring a belief in the usefulness – also the reality – of the moral progress towards true architecture. An architecture that genuinely expresses itself between the assertion of the old, reliable values and the exploration of the new in the spirit of the time, as we have always experienced it with Renzo Piano. The task is clear. We should open up buildings more forcefully and permeate them with creative integration, making them into a contemporary architecture of timeless beauty and self-evidence.

It could be wrong to see architecture only in a context with originality. It is not about "gestalt invention", rather it is more about "finding the gestalt". The true and independent can be found. Or, as Mies van der Rohe put it: "I want the form and not a formal play". If this sentence is taken seriously, one will see architecture where it truly wants to be pure gestalt.

Renzo Piano's own world view is always connected with general creativity: with the origin of nature and the natural. The creative idea is expressed in the "divine intuition" and also in spontaneous decision or intuitive awareness. The creative is akin to playful activity. Even the origin of creativity is found in play, requiring one to be self motivated, free to set one's own goals, as well as having the opportunity for free reflection.

Gestaltsuche und Gestaltfindung

Der wahrheitshaltige Sinn des Kulturzentrums läßt uns ahnen, daß durch Denken Qualität entsteht. Kriterien können sich dadurch neu ordnen. Im Verstehen wird wahrgenommen und so entwickelt sich ein meditatives Denken, in dem die schöpferische Kraft auch wurzelt. Die Suche nach der Vereinfachung wird bei jedem ernstzunehmenden Architekten zu einer eigentlichen Herausforderung. Reduzieren auf das Elementare. Darin liegt Glückseligkeit. Mit dieser Lehre zu arbeiten und damit auch in anderen Kulturen Architektur zu realisieren bedeutet, auch neue Zusammenhänge zu finden und zu formulieren.
Eine Station auf dieser Suche nach hohem künstlerischen Anspruch bleibt, jene wirkliche Gestalt zu finden, mit der durch geringsten Aufwand an Material und Masse ein Bauwerk formiert wird. Unabhängig von der Festlegung durch ein einfaches Material- und Konstruktionssystem werden die Holzwerk-Lamellenwände von der Schönheit und Harmonie ihrer Proportionen geprägt. Die großen Vorzüge einer inszenierten Ordnung bestehen darin, daß die Ästhetik eines Gebäudes durch die klaren Prinzipien reguliert wird. Zugleich geht es darum, einen Ort (wieder) mit Magie zu erfüllen.
In der Transformation der schöpferischen Kraft liegt das Maß der inneren Wahrhaftigkeit. Es ist eine harmonische Art des Wirkens, im Einklang mit der Kanak-Kultur und mit dem Gegenwärtigen. Die ganze Kreation wird zum Mitschwingen gebracht. Der Durchbruch vollzieht sich dann bei jedem Element, das sich in seiner Art entfaltet. Man sagt: «Was im Ton übereinstimmt, schwingt miteinander». Hier trifft das ganz besonders in der Profilierung des Holzes zu. Es ist verständlich, daß man sich von der magischen Wirkung reduzierter Architekturgestalt angezogen fühlt.

Anspruch und Haltung

Mit der Schaffung eines kulturellen Wahrzeichens, bei dem die traditionelle Rundhütte der Kanak Pate stand, wurde ein Juwel der Weltarchitektur kreiert. Dieses Zurückgreifen auf bestehende Bau-Traditionen half mit, eine Gebäudesequenz mit außerordentlichen, komplexen Funktionen in Holztechnologie zu entwickeln. Die regional vorgegebenen Grundlagen, zusammen mit den technologischen Möglichkeiten unserer Zeit, brachten die Topographie in Beziehung zu diesem Wahrzeichen einer neuen Architektur. Hohe Anforderungen, vollständig in die räumliche Situation umgesetzt, ergeben die Schönheit des Kulturzentrums. Zum Zukunftsweisenden dieser Architektur gehört auch der Gesamtauftritt einer Bauaufgabe. Es geht dabei darum, im Erscheinungsbild den Anspruch im Sinne einer Corporate Identity zu verdeutlichen.

Searching and Finding the Gestalt

The truthful sense of the J. M. Tjibaou cultural center gives us a feeling for the fact that quality is created as a result of reflection through which criteria is able to find new order. We perceive in the process of understanding, and thus a meditative reflection develops in which the creative force is rooted. The search for simplification becomes a true challenge with every serious architect. Reduction to the elemental. Therein lies bliss. Working with this teaching and using it to realize architecture in other cultures means to find and formulate new contexts.

One vital aspect that remains constant during this search for a high artistic standard, is to find that real gestalt with which a building is formed through the least expenditure in material and mass. The wooden lamellar walls, independent from determination through a simple material and construction system, are characterized by the beauty and harmony of their proportions. The big advantages of a staged order are that the aesthetics of a building are regulated by the clear principles. At the same time, it is about instilling a location with magic.

In the transformation of the creative power lies the measure of inner truthfulness. It is a harmonic kind of activity, in harmony with the Kanak culture and the present. The entire creation is put into vibration. The breakthrough happens with every element that unfolds in its kind. They say: "Whatever is in accord in the atmosphere vibrates together". This applies here, especially to the profile of the wood. It is understandable that one feels attracted to the magical effect of the reduced architectural gestalt.

Standard and Attitude

With the creation of a cultural emblem to which the traditional round hut of the Kanak is a godfather, a jewel of the world's architecture was created. This resorting to existing building traditions assisted in the development of a sequence of buildings with exceptional, complicated functions in wood technology. The regionally stipulated foundations, together with the technological possibilities of our time, put the topography into a relationship with this emblem of a new architecture. High standards, realized into the spatial situation without any waste products, resulted in the beauty of the cultural center. The trendsetting character of this architecture is a necessary part of its presentation, which is about clarifying the standard of the appearance in the sense of a corporate identity.

Hütten-Pavillons

Neukaledonien (etwa 400 km lang und 40 km breit) ist eine der vielen Inseln im südlichen Pazifik, östlich von Australien und nördlich von Neuseeland gelegen. Es ist ein französisches überseeisches Territorium, in dem die kanakische Urbevölkerung noch heute lebt. Der Name «Kanak» verweist auf das ozeanische Grundwort für «Mensch». Für ein Kulturzentrum der Kanak auf dem Ufergelände einer Lagune, etwas außerhalb der Stadt Nouméa, wurde ein internationaler Wettbewerb auf Einladungsbasis ausgeschrieben. Zur Realisierung einer Dorfanlage, wie die Sippenverbände der Kanak sie bewohnen, wurden auch Wissenschaftler, Anthropologen und Ethnographen zur Ideensammlung eingeladen.

Renzo Piano gewann 1991 diesen Wettbewerb, weil er sich in das Denken der Kanak einzufühlen versuchte, die im Einklang mit der Natur leben. In ehrlicher Anerkennung des Vergangenen hat Piano seine neuentworfenen Hütten mit der einheimischen Tradition verbunden, ins Heute übersetzt und mit der Gestalt seiner Pavillons auch auf den vom Pazifik wehenden, starken Wind konstruktiv reagiert. Die zehn segmentartigen Türme mit der kreisförmigen Basis, die an das heimische Rundhaus erinnern, dienen verschiedenen Bestimmungen, wie Mediathek, Seminarräume, Ausstellungen, Cafeteria. Davor sind die einstöckigen, flachen Verwaltungsbauten, die sich am Hang auch mehrstöckig entfalten, sowie ein Auditorium für 400 Personen.

Mit nur zwei Materialien, dem natürlich-unbehandelten, zähen Irokoholz in laminierter Konstruktion und in Form von Stäben in der Lamellenverkleidung sowie den – statisch notwendigen – verzinkten Stahlplatten und -rohren, wurde das Meisterwerk realisiert. Die 2 cm starken und 45 cm breiten vernickelten Stahlflachteile sind beidseitig mit 6 cm dicken laminierten Holzteilen als Sandwichelemente verstärkt.

Die eigenwillige Skyline der zehn Pavillons mit filigranen Masten, die hoch über den Mangrovenwald ragt, überrascht und beeindruckt durch ihre strahlende Präsenz. Die Pavillons sind ein Zentrum geworden für das kulturelle Selbstverständnis der Kanak und das Bewußtwerden ihrer gemeinsamen Wurzeln.

Hut Pavilions

New Caledonia (about 400 km long and 40 km wide) is one of the many islands in the south Pacific, east of Australia and north of New Zealand. It is a French territory where the native Kanak population still lives today. The name "Kanak" refers to the oceanic word for "human being". An international invitational competition was held for a Kanak cultural center to be situated on the shore of a lagoon, just outside the city of Nouméa. Scientists, anthropologists and ethnographers were also invited to gather ideas for the realization of a village compound like those that the Kanak tribes inhabit.

Renzo Piano won this competition in 1991 because of his endeavor to empathize with the Kanak, who live in harmony with nature. In an honest attempt to give recognition to the past, Piano combined his newly designed huts with the native tradition, translating them into the present in a way that constructively reacted to the strong wind blowing in from the Pacific. The ten segment-like towers, with a circular base reminiscent of the local roundhouse, serve various purposes such as a media library, seminar rooms, exhibitions, and cafeteria. The one-story flat administrative buildings that unfold on the slope over several levels, and an auditorium for 400 people are situated in front of them.

The masterpiece was realized with just two materials: the natural, untreated and very sturdy Iroko wood in both a laminated construction and as rods in the lamella cladding, and the – statically necessary – galvanized steel sheets and tubes. The galvanized steel panels are 2 cm thick and 45 cm wide and are sandwiched on both sides with 6 cm thick laminated wood parts as reinforcement.

The very individual skyline of the ten pavilions with filigree masts rising high above the mangrove forest surprises and impresses with its shining presence. The pavilions have become a center for the cultural self-image of the Kanak as well as a focal point for the coming into awareness of their common roots.

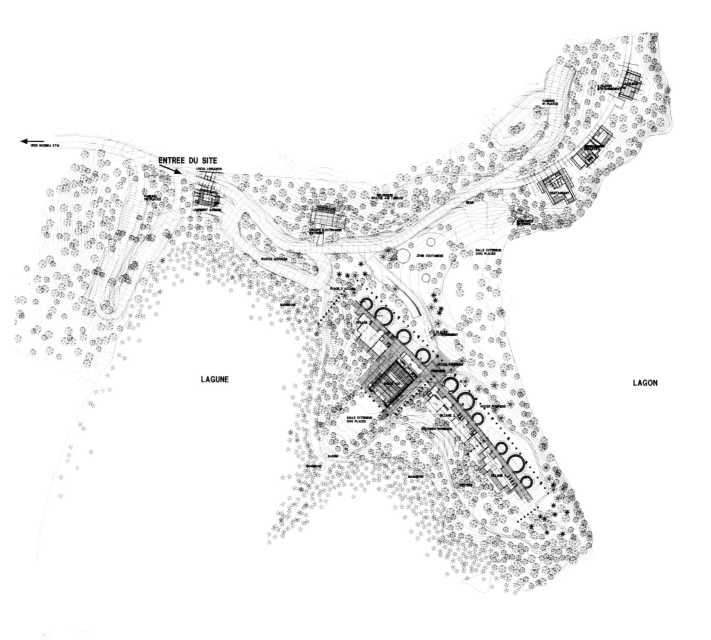

VERS NOUMÉA ET 14

ENTRÉE DU SITE

LAGUNE

LAGON

Über Renzo Piano

Wahre Architektur verbindet Aufgabe und Ort. Renzo Piano besitzt die Begabung, seine Bauwerke aus den programmatischen Voraussetzungen heraus und unter Berücksichtigung der örtlichen Gegebenheiten zu entwickeln. Sein Stil ist Wandlung und Anpassung, entwickelt aus der Basis der Wahrheit des Entwurfs. Das Repertoire der Details kann sich wiederholen und wird meisterlich der gegebenen Situation angepaßt. Das Erfinderische im Neuen braucht Intellekt; Pianos Stärke ist die Analyse der jeweiligen Aufgabe.

Seine Firma nennt er «Renzo Piano Building Workshop», mit seinen Bauten möchte er den Anspruch des baumeisterlichen Metiers ausweisen. Seine Modelle – bis hin zum natürlichen Maßstab 1:1 – sind Zeugen eines Baumeisters. Hinzu kommt Renzo Pianos kosmopolitisches Auftreten. Er verknüpft die Wirkungskraft seines Büros am Rande von Genua, seiner Geburtsstadt, mit den Leistungen seines Ateliers in Paris zu einer weltweit ausgreifenden Tätigkeit. Seine mediterrane Ausstrahlung ist in seinem Innern fest verankert und ist seine persönliche Auszeichnung.

About Renzo Piano

True architecture combines the task and the location. Renzo Piano has the talent to develop his buildings in accordance with the programmatic stipulations and in consideration of the local situation. His style is change and adjustment, developed from the basic truth of the design. The repertoire of the details can repeat itself and is masterfully adjusted to the existing situation. The inventive in the new requires intellect; Piano's strength is the analysis of each task.

He calls his company "Renzo Piano Building Workshop", and with his buildings he wants to express the standards of the architectural profession. His models – to the natural scale 1:1 – are witnesses of a master builder. Added to that is Renzo Piano's cosmopolitan appearance. He combines both the efficacy of his office on the outskirts of Genova, his native town, and the achievements of his studio in Paris into a global activity. His Mediterranean charisma, which is firmly anchored, is his personal mark of distinction.

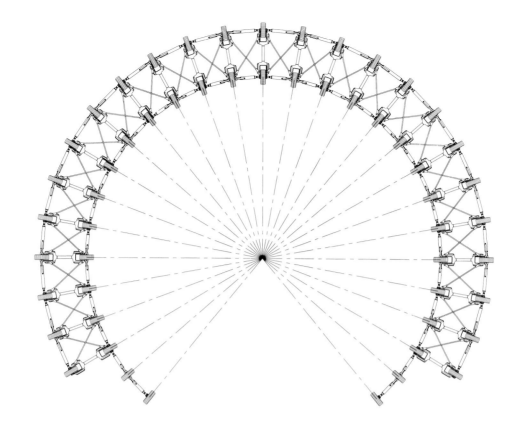

28

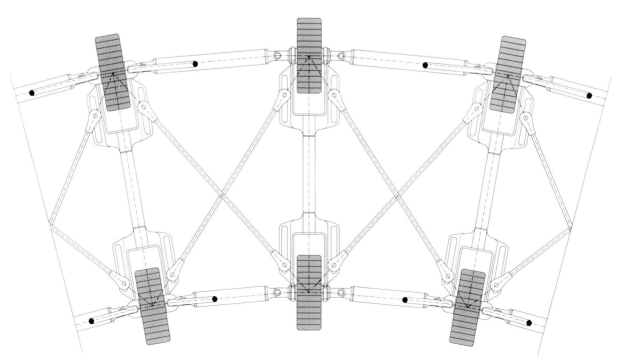

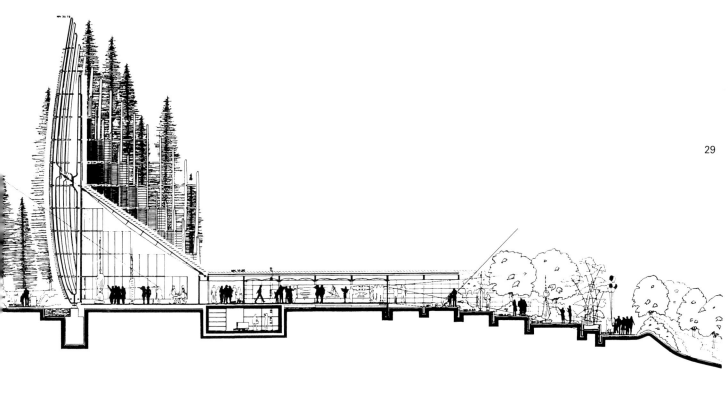

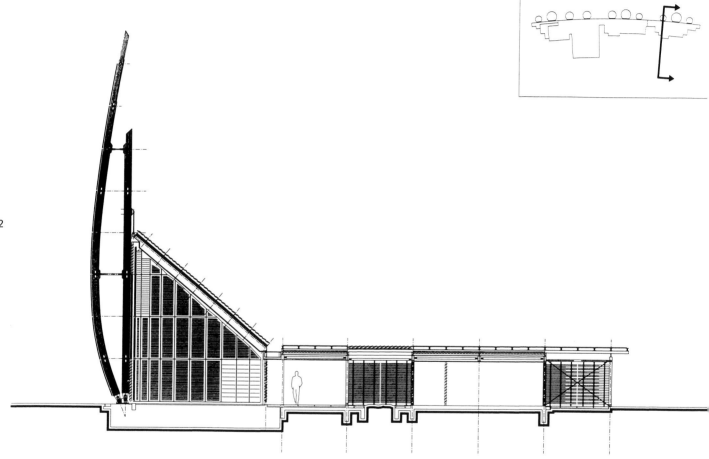

3

4

2

1

Flachbauten

Ein großer Wandel ist bei Renzo Piano vom Centre Pompidou in Paris, einer Zusammenarbeit mit Richard Rogers 1971–77 in High-tech-Manier, bis zum Kulturzentrum J. M. Tjibaou in Nouméa, 1993–99 in Holz-tech-Ausführung, wahrnehmbar. Die neue Vorgehensweise mit Holz-tech geht auf drei Aspekte zurück. Die Holzlamination vermag den starken Windansturm zu bändigen und schafft so eine natürliche Klimatisierung im Innern. Zudem besitzt Holz die Erfahrbarkeit von Nähe und natürliche Ausstrahlung. Im Prozeß des Laminierens, den eine spezialisierte Werkstatt im Elsaß ausführte, wird Beständigkeit und Dauerhaftigkeit erzeugt. Dazu war das wetterbeständige Irokoholz aus Java besonders geeignet. Zusammen mit den Ingenieuren von Ove Arup hatte der Renzo Piano Building Workshop im Windkanal experimentiert. In Nouméa kann ein Monsun Geschwindigkeiten von bis zu 200 km/h erreichen. Das technologisch abgesicherte Gebilde ist bis heute vollkommen stabil, wie Emmanuel Kasarhérou, Directeur Culturel am J. M. Tjibaou-Zentrum, bestätigt. Durch eine 24stündige Computerüberwachung werden die Glaslamellen der inneren Fassade automatisch geöffnet oder geschlossen. Die äußeren Lamellen der Holzfassade hingegen sind fest. Die Metallfassade, die den Innenraum bestimmt, ist im Abstand von 120 cm zur äußeren Holzkonstruktion montiert. Konstruktive Verstrebungen zwischen den beiden Fassaden sind aus nichtrostendem Metall gefertigt. Besonders eindrücklich ist die Kreativität im Umgang mit den Möglichkeiten der Holztechnologie: Holz-tech als ein großartiges Zusammenführen von Technik und Ästhetik.

Ethnologen und Anthropologen haben mit dem Architekten zusammen das Wesen der einheimischen Bauten, wie etwa das Unfertige und Prozeßhafte, umgesetzt. Die oben offene Muschelform der Pavillons von 22 und 28 m Höhe ist somit von der Tradition inspiriert, aber zugleich ein Symbol für das neu Entstehende. Die waagrechten Holzlamellen bei den aufstrebenden Masten der kreisförmigen Türme erinnern ebenfalls an das Flechtwerk der traditionellen Konstruktionsweisen. Dieses Gitterwerk dient auch dem ausgeklügelten natürlichen Lüftungssystem. Der starke Wind, der durch die verstellbaren computergesteuerten Lamellen im Zwischenraum von Hülle und Innenwand eindringt, führt die warme Luft nach oben.

Das Centre Kanak ist auf den ersten Anhieb nicht als eigentliches Gebäude erkennbar. In die rechenartig aufstrebenden, hohen Türme ist auf Raumhöhe ein Pultdach gelegt. Angeschlossen sind Flachbauten, gegen den Hang mehrstöckig, die der Administration und als Ausstellungsräume dienen. Eine fragile Stahlskelettkonstruktion, die elegant mit der Holz-tech-Ästhetik der Türme verbunden ist und geradezu paradigmatisch zu einer herausragenden Architektur unserer Zeit geworden ist.

Low-rise Buildings

A big change can be perceived in Renzo Piano's work from Centre Pompidou in Paris, a collaboration with Richard Rogers 1971–77 in a high-tech manner, to the cultural center J. M. Tjibaou in Nouméa, 1993–99 in a wood-tech version. The new procedure with wood-tech goes back to three aspects. The wood lamination has the ability to tame the strong winds, thus creating natural ventilation in the interior. Wood also incorporates characteristics including the experience of closeness and natural radiation. The resulting longevity and durability are a product of the lamination process done by a specialized factory in Alsace. The weather-resistant Iroko wood from Java was especially suited for this purpose. Together with the engineers from Ove Arup, the Renzo Piano Building Workshop conducted experiments in a wind tunnel. In Nouméa, monsoon winds can reach speeds of up to 200 km/hr. The technologically secured shape is completely stable to this day, as Emmanuel Kasarhérou, Directeur cultural at J. M. Tjibaou Center confirms. The glass louvers of the inner façade are automatically opened or closed through 24-hour computer monitoring. The outer lamellas of the wood façade, however, are solid. The metal façade determining the interior is assembled at a distance of 120 cm to the outer wood construction. Constructive struts between the two facades are made of stainless metal. The creativity with which the new possibilities of wood technology were handled is especially impressive, resulting in a wood-tech that is a grand unification of technology and aesthetics.

Ethnologists and anthropologists realized the essence of the local buildings, its unfinished and process-like qualities, together with the architect. The shell form of the pavilions, with a height of 22 and 28 meters, is open towards the top and is thus inspired by tradition, while at the same time serving as a symbol for the new. The horizontal wood lamellae on the rising masts of the circular towers also remind us of the weavings found in traditional construction methods. This gridwork also serves the sophisticated natural ventilation system. The strong wind that enters into the space between the shell and inner wall through the adjustable computer controlled louvers, move the warm air to the top.

At first sight, Centre Kanak is not recognizable as an actual building. At ceiling level, a shed roof was put into the high, raked towers. Flat buildings adjoin with several floors towards the slope housing the administration and exhibition spaces. A fragile steel skeletal structure elegantly connected with the wood-tech aesthetics of the towers has almost paradigmatically become an outstanding architecture of our time.

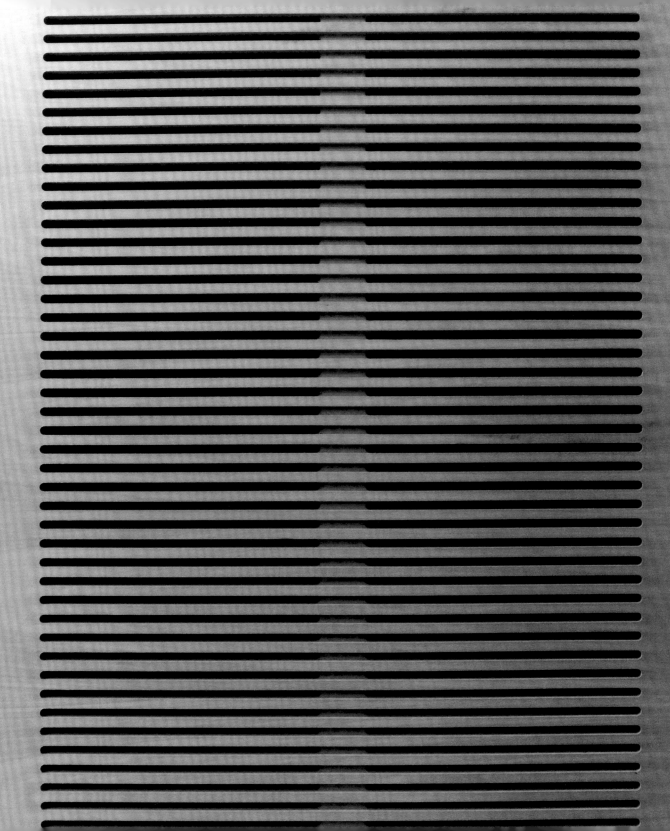

Chemin Kanak

Im Kulturzentrum in Nouméa öffnet Renzo Piano den Raum zur Landschaft, zum Himmel und zum Licht. Im Spiel des Lichts entfalten sich hell und dunkel, aber auch Schärfe und Weichheit der Konturen. Licht bringt Stimmung und Wirkung, Offenheit und Großzügigkeit, weckt aber auch die Phantasie. Der Architekt Louis Kahn sagte: «Am Kreuzpunkt von Stille und Licht liegt das Heiligtum der Kunst, diese einzigartige Sprache des Menschen. Es ist eine Schatzkammer der Schatten. Unsere Bauten sind Schaffenswerke und gehören dem Licht.»

Sinnfällige Gestalt muß sich auf ein «Mehr» einlassen – ein Credo für Renzo Piano. Den Anspruch auf sinnfällige Menschlichkeit finden wir in der Lichtqualität, in Material und Konstruktion, im technischen System, in der räumlichen Gestalt verwirklicht.

Im Kulturzentrum ist Architektur gebaute Umwelt. In der Gestalt finden wir die Ganzheit von Material und Konstruktion sowie Harmonie und Proportion als genuinen Anspruch an die Schönheit. In der Logik der Konstruktion entsteht sinnvolles Fügen mit Holz und Stahl und Sichtbarmachen der ihr eigenen Möglichkeiten und Grenzen. Aus diesen Grundgedanken wird das räumliche Milieu mitbestimmt. Im klaren Fügen – wir denken hier etwa an die Holz-Metall-Sandwichkonstruktion der Stützen – liegt das Finden einer sinnfälligen Gestalt.

Der «Chemin Kanak» ist eine Art Meditationsweg, auf dem die Besucher die enge Anlehnung an die Naturauffassung der Kanak erleben. Man findet dort zum Beispiel zwischen den Mangrovenbäumen die großen Säulen-Pinien – den Baum, der zum Haus jedes Stammeschefs gehört. Somit wird die reiche Vegetation der Südseeinsel ein Teil des Centre und agiert im wechselseitigen Spiel zwischen Gebautem und Gewachsenem.

Chemin Kanak

Renzo Piano has opened the space of the cultural center in Nouméa to the landscape, the sky and the light. In the play of the light, not only do lightness and darkness unfold, but also the sharpness and softness of the contours. Light provides an atmosphere and effect that inspires openness and generosity, as well as fantasy. The architect Louis Kahn said: "At the crossroads of silence and light lies the relic of art, this unique language of mankind. It is a treasury of shadows. Our buildings are creations and belong to the light".

Obvious gestalt has to let itself in for "more" – a creed for Renzo Piano. The standard for obvious humaneness can be found as realized in the quality of the light, the material and construction, the technical system and the spatial design.

For the cultural center, architecture is a constructed environment. In the design, we find the wholeness of material and construction as well as harmony and proportion, as a genuine standard of beauty. In the logic of the construction, a sensible joining of wood and steel has not only been created, but its own possibilities and limitations have also been made visible. The spatial milieu has also been determined by this principle idea. The clear joinery – for example, consider the wood-metal sandwich construction of the supports – implies the finding of an obvious gestalt.

The "Chemin Kanak" is a kind of meditative pathway upon which the visitors experience the close connection of the concept of nature to the Kanak. For example, the large pine trees can be found between the mangrove trees, the tree that is part of the house of every tribal chief. The rich vegetation of the South Seas Island thus becomes a part of the Center, interacting in the play between the constructed and the naturally grown.

68

TO: DATE :

ATT: FAX :

CC: FAX :

CC: FAX :

TOTAL PAGES (including this page) :

FROM

PROJECT: NOUMEA - TJIBAOU CULTURAL CENTER -

SUBJECT:

- WE ENCLOSED THE ANSWER OF YOUR QUESTION ABOUT THE CRITERIA FOR SPECIFYING THE "IROKO" TIMBER IN THE PROJECT OF THE "TJIBAOU CULTURAL CENTER".

- THERE WAS FIVE MAIN CRITERIA TO CHOOSE WICH WOOD TO USE.

- 1 - NO MAINTENANCE. (FOR THE WOOD)

THIS WAS VERY IMPORTANT FOR RENZO PIANO. HE WANT THAT THE BUILDING GROW OLD IN THE BEST CONDITIONS, AND AS IT IS A "COMPLEX" BUILDING, FACING THE OCEAN, DROWNED IN THE VEGETATION, HE SAID THAT THE BUILDING MUST BE ABLE TO "PROTECT HINSELF" BECAUSE THERE WILL HAVE NOBODY (AND NO MONEY !!!) TO REPAINT THE ALL WOOD EACH FIVE YEARS...
AS THE IROKO WOOD (TREE) GROW UP IN AN EARTH

WITH A LOT OF HYDROCARBON, IT PUMP THE HYDROCARBON DURING ALL HIS LIFE AND THEN, WHEN YOU CUT THE TREE, IT'S "FULL" OF HYDROCARBON.
THIS HYDROCARBON WILL MAKE THE WOOD A LITTLE BIT "FAT", AND IT WILL PROTECT THE WOOD.
SO THE WOOD IT PROTECT BY HINSELF, DON'T NEED ANY MAINTENANCE !

- 2 - WOOD WHICH IS ABLE TO BE GLULANS .

AS THE HUT ARE VERY HIGHT (20, 22 AND 28 METERS) RENZO DECIDED TO USE GLULANS TECHNOLOGY, BECAUSE HE WANTED HIS BUILDING IN WOOD. BUT THERE WAS AN OTHER PROBLEM, IT WAS THE CYCLONE... WITH A 240 KN/H WIND, SO WE ALSO NEED A WOOD WHICH IS VERY "STRONG", VERY RESISTANT.
THE IROKO WOOD CAN BE GLULANS AND IT'S VERY RESISTANT.

- 3 - THE WAY THAT THE WOOD (BUILDING ALSO...) LOOK WHEN OLD.

RENZO PIANO WAS VERY ATTACHED TO THE WAY THAT THE WOOD WILL GROW OLD. HE WANTED TO KOW HOW WILL BE THE BUILDING IN 5, 10 AND 100 YEARS!!! SO EACH TIME THAT THE BUILDING TEAM (R.P.B.WS ARCHITECTS) PROPOSED A WOOD, WE DID HAVE TO BE ABLE TO SHOW THE WAY IT LOOK WHEN IT'S OLD.

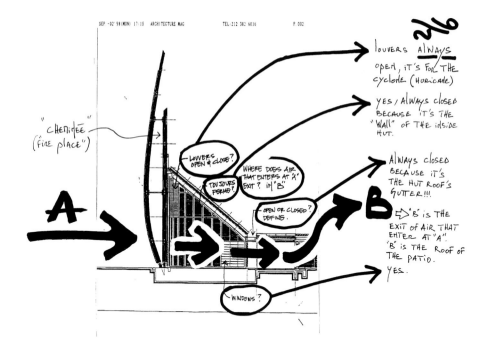

"CHEMIÉE"
(FIRE PLACE)

A →

B

- LOUVERS
OPEN & CLOSE?
- TOUJOURS
FERMÉ?

WHERE DOES AIR
THAT ENTERS AT "A"
EXIT? IN "B"

OPEN OR CLOSED?
DEFINE.

WINDOWS?

LOUVERS ALWAYS
OPEN, IT'S FOR THE
cyclone (HURICANE)

YES, ALWAYS CLOSED
BECAUSE IT'S THE
"WALL" OF THE INSIDE
HUT.

ALWAYS CLOSED
BECAUSE IT'S
THE HUT ROOF'S
GUTTER!!!

⇨ "B" IS THE
EXIT OF AIR THAT
ENTER AT "A".
"B" IS THE ROOF OF
THE PATIO.

YES.

Renzo Piano Building Workshop
Via P.P. Rubens, 29 - 16158 Genova
tel. 010/61711 - fax 010/6171.350
e-mail : renzopianobwit@panet.it

RENZO PIANO WAS "AFRAID" THAT HIS BUILDING LOOK
LIKE A SERIAL OF "SWISS CHALET/COUNTRY COTTAGE" WITH
A LOT OF WOOD VERY WELL VARNISH.
HE WANT A WOOD WHICH WAS "FRUGAL", "RUGOSE" AND
WITH A SOFT COLOUR.
AS THE IROKO WOOD DON'T NEED ANY MAINTENANCE,
IT STAY "FRUGAL AND RUGOSE" AND WHEN IT BECOME
OLD HIS COLOUR IS CLOSE TO WHITE-GREY (SAME
COLOUR THAT THE COCONUT'S TRUNK). RENZO LIKE IT !

-4- "TERMITE PROOF."

AS IN MANY PART OF THE WORLD, THERE IS A LOT OF
TERMITE IN NEW-CALEDONIA, SO WE NEED A WOOD
WHICH WAS "TERMITE PROOF".
THE IROKO WOOD IS TERMITE PROOF.

-5- THE VALUE ($) AND THE CONCURRENCE.

THIS FIFTH CRITERIA ARRIVED A LITTLE BIT LATER
THAN THE OTHER, BECAUSE, IN FACT WE DIDN'T THING
ABOUT IT BEFORE BECOMING ASKING PRICE TO
DIFFERENTS SUPPLIERS.
THE PROBLEM WAS THAT WE FOUND DIFFERENT WOOD
WHICH WERE "OK" WITH POINTS 1,2,3 é 4 BUT SOME OF

Renzo Piano Building Workshop
Via P.P. Rubens, 29 - 16158 Genova
tel. 010/61711 - fax 010/6171.350
e-mail : renzopianobwit@panet.it

THEM (LIKE KOHU, HOUP...) WERE PRODUCED IN ONLY
ONE COUNTRY, SO THERE WASN'T ANY POSSIBLE
CONCURRENCE!!! WE COULDN'T CHECK THE VALUE !!!
THE IROKO WOOD IS PRODUCT IN DIFFERENTS
COUNTRYS (THE ONE WHICH WAS USE FOR US
IS COMING FROM GHANA), AND IT IS PLANTED
TO BE CUT, IT IS IN AN ECONOMIC LOGICAL.

-CONCLUSION-

THE IROKO TIMBER WAS THE ONLY WOOD OK
WITH POINTS 1,2,3,4 é 5...

- IF YOU HAVE ANY OTHER QUESTIONS, PLEASE DO
NOT HESITATE TO CONTACT US.
FOR RENZO PIANO BUILDING WORKSHOP, ARCHITECTS:

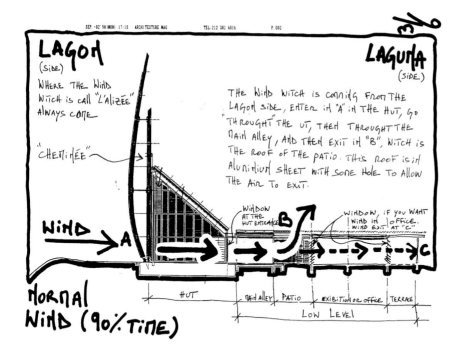

LAGON
(SIDE)

WHERE THE WIND WITCH IS CALL "L'ALIZEE" ALWAYS COME

"CHEMINEE"

WIND ➤ A

NORMAL WIND (90% TIME)

LAGUNA
(SIDE)

THE WIND WITCH IS COMING FROM THE LAGON SIDE, ENTER IN "A" IN THE HUT, GO THROUGHT THE UT, THEN THROUGHT THE MAIN ALLEY, AND THEN EXIT IN "B", WITCH IS THE ROOF OF THE PATIO. THIS ROOF IS IN ALUMINIUM SHEET WITH SOME HOLE TO ALLOW THE AIR TO EXIT.

WINDOW AT THE HUT ENTRANCE   B

WINDOW, IF YOU WANT WIND IN OFFICE. WIND EXIT AT "C"   C

HUT | MAIN ALLEY | PATIO | EXHIBITION OR OFFICE | TERRACE
LOW LEVEL

70

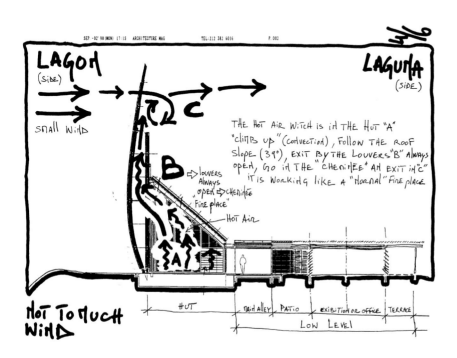

LAGON
(SIDE)

SMALL WIND

LAGUNA
(SIDE)

C

B
➤ LOUVERS ALWAYS OPEN ➤ CHEMINEE "FIRE PLACE"
HOT AIR
A

THE HOT AIR WITCH IS IN THE HUT "A" "CLIMB UP" (CONVECTION), FOLLOW THE ROOF SLOPE (39°), EXIT BY THE LOUVERS "B" ALWAYS OPEN, GO IN THE "CHEMINEE" AN EXIT IN "C" IT IS WORKING LIKE A "NORMAL" FIRE PLACE

HOT TO MUCH WIND

HUT | MAIN ALLEY | PATIO | EXHIBITION OR OFFICE | TERRACE
LOW LEVEL

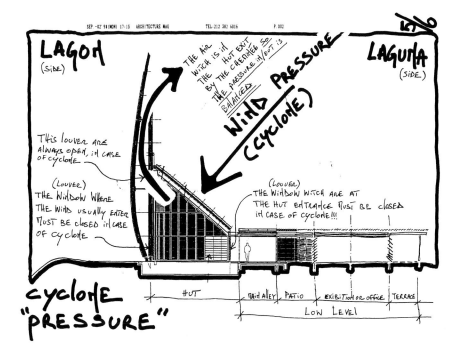

LAGON (side)

THE AIR WITCH IS IN THE HUT EXIT THE CHENNEE SO BY THE PRESSURE IN/OUT IS <u>BALANCED</u>

WIND PRESSURE (CYCLONE)

LAGUNA (side)

This louver are always open, in case of cyclone

(Louver) THE WINDOW WHERE THE WIND USUALLY ENTER MUST BE CLOSED IN CASE OF CYCLONE

(LOUVER) THE WINDOW WITCH ARE AT THE HUT ENTRANCE MUST BE CLOSED IN CASE OF CYCLONE!!!

CYCLONE "PRESSURE"

HUT | MAIN ALLEY | PATIO | EXIBITION OR OFFICE | TERRACE

LOW LEVEL

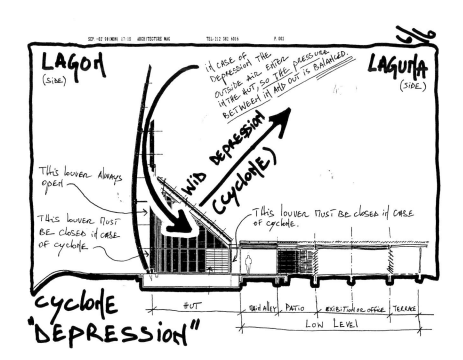

LAGON (side)

IN CASE OF DEPRESSION THE OUTSIDE AIR ENTER IN THE HUT, SO THE PRESSURE BETWEEN IN AND OUT IS <u>BALANCED</u>.

WIND DEPRESSION (CYCLONE)

LAGUNA (side)

This louver ALWAYS OPEN

This louver MUST BE CLOSED IN CASE OF cyclone

This louver MUST BE CLOSED IN CASE OF cyclone.

CYCLONE "DEPRESSION"

HUT | MAIN ALLEY | PATIO | EXIBITION OR OFFICE | TERRACE

LOW LEVEL

Dank

Mit Ausnahme des Vorsatzfotos und der Fotos auf den Seiten 6 und 7 (S. Gollings) stammen alle vom Verfasser. Die Zeichnungen sind aus «La Maison Kanak», Editions Parenthèses 1990, entnommen. Renzo Piano und seinem Sekretariat gebührt für die Planbeschaffung aufrichtiger Dank. Der Basler Ethnologe Dr. Christian Kaufmann hat in mir das Verständnis für das Centre Kanak in Nouméa geweckt und die Verbindung hergestellt. Der dortige Directeur Culturel, Dr. Emmanuel Kasarhérou, hat mich in dieses bedeutende kulturelle Zentrum mit Feinfühligkeit eingeführt. Eine Bereicherung ist auch die Eröffnungsrede von Madame Marie-Claude Tjibaou. Ihnen allen sei herzlich gedankt.

Credits

All pictures were taken by the author, except those on flyleaf and on pages 6 and 7 (S. Gollings). The drawings are taken from "La Maison Kanak", Editions Parenthèses 1990. My sincere thanks go to Renzo Piano and his office for providing the plans. The Basel ethnologist, Dr. Christian Kaufmann, roused my awareness of the Centre Kanak in Nouméa and established the connection with the center. The Directeur Culturel of Centre Kanak, Dr. Emmanuel Kasarhérou, has introduced me with great sensitivity to this important cultural center. The inaugural address by Madame Marie-Claude Tjibaou is a valuable addition. My heartfelt gratitude goes to all of them.

Eröffnungsrede von Madame Marie-Claude Tjibaou zur Einweihung des
Centre Culturel Tjibaou am 4. Mai 1998

Sehr geehrter Herr Premierminister,

Frau Minister,

Herr Staatssekretär,

Herr Abgesandter der Regierung,

meine Damen und Herren Regierungsvertreter der Länder Ozeaniens,

Herr Senator,

meine Damen und Herren Abgeordneten,

Herr Kongreßpräsident,

meine Herren Provinzpräsidenten,

Herr Bürgermeister von Nouméa, meine Herren Bürgermeister,

meine Herren Vertreter der traditionellen Autoritäten,

meine Herren Präsidenten des FLNKS und des RPCR,

liebe Freunde,

erlauben Sie mir, Herr Premierminister, Ihnen zu danken, daß Sie unserer Einladung mit solcher Herzlichkeit gefolgt sind, denn Ihre Anwesenheit unterstreicht den nationalen Rang des Centre Culturel Tjibaou und macht deutlich, was auf dem Spiel steht.

Wenn wir an diesem Datum festgehalten haben, obwohl die Bauarbeiten kaum erst abgeschlossen sind, so vor allem, weil es der Todestag von Jean-Marie Tjibaou und Yéiwéné Yéiwéné ist. Doch das Ereignis, an dem wir heute teilhaben, ist weit mehr als eine bloße Gedenkfeier. In der Tat fällt die Fertigstellung des Kulturzentrums mit dem Abschluß der Verhandlungen zusammen, die bei den Vereinbarungen von Matignon beschlossen wurden, und es wird am gleichen Tag eingeweiht, an dem die Vereinbarungen von Nouméa unterzeichnet werden, die eine neue Phase in der Geschichte unseres Landes einleiten. Die heutige Einweihung dieses Zentrums setzt ein unübersehbares Zeichen im Geist von Jean-Marie Tjibaou.

Bei den Verhandlungen in der Rue Oudinot hatte Jean-Marie Wert darauf gelegt, daß die «Agence de Développement de la Culture Kanak» (A.D.C.K., dt: «Organisation zur Entwicklung der Kanak-Kultur») geschaffen wurde, um die Kultur der Kanak zu verbreiten, weil wir, wie er sagte, «der Welt mitteilen wollen, daß wir keine Überlebenden aus der Vorgeschichte und noch weniger archäologische Überbleibsel sind, sondern Menschen aus Fleisch und Blut». Er hat dieser Organisation die Aufgabe zugedacht, die Kultur der Kanak als Erbe zu bewahren, aber auch auf ihre Aktualität und ihre zeitgenössischen Hervorbringungen hinzuweisen. Er hat die Zusage für ein Gelände in Nouméa erhalten, auf dem diese Institution errichtet werden konnte. Er hat diesem großen Projekt von Anfang an die Richtung gewiesen: den maßgeblichen Beitrag der Kanak-Kultur zur Identität dieses Landes darzustellen.

Inaugural address by Madame Marie-Claude Tjibaou at the opening of the
Centre Culturel Tjibaou on 4 May 1998

The Prime Minister
The Minister
The Secretary of State
The Government Representative
The Government Representatives of the South Pacific
The Senator
The Members of Parliament
The Chairman of Congress
The Chairmen of the Provinces
The Mayors , The Mayor of Noumea
The Representatives of the cultural authorities
The Chairmen of FLNKS and of RPCR
Friends

First of all, thank you most sincerely Prime Minister for having responded so warmly to our invitation. Being here today illustrates just how important you believe the Tjibaou Cultural Center to be.
Our reason for choosing today as the opening – even though construction is barely finished – is because it is the anniversary of the deaths of Jean-Marie Tjibaou and Yéiwéné Yéiwéné. Yet this ceremony is much more than a simple commemoration, for the completion of the Cultural Center coincides both with the end of the Matignon agreement and with the signing of the Noumea accord, which marks a new chapter in the history of our country. In short, the inauguration of the Center today is a key event embodying the spirit of Jean-Marie Tjibaou.
At the time of the Oudinot agreement, Jean-Marie decided to set up the "Agence de Développement de la Culture Kanak" (A.D.C.K., "Agency for the Development of Kanak Culture"), for as he said: "We wish to tell the world that we are not prehistoric survivors, nor are we archaeological remains. We are people of flesh and blood". By obtaining a plot of land in Noumea on which to build this Agency and by entrusting it with the task of promoting not only the heritage but also the modern creative aspects of Kanak culture, Jean-Marie was mapping out the philosophy underpinning the Center. It is a philosophy rooted in resolutely inscribing Kanak culture in Noumea with a view to providing a common source of identity. By offering Kanak heritage as a cultural legacy for the whole population of New Caledonia, and by developing artistic creation, the following aims can be achieved:
– Kanaks – both young and old – will proudly rediscover their roots
– Non-Kanaks will share a South Pacific identity and cultural references, enabling them to help develop new cultural practices

Das Erbe der Kanak der ganzen Bevölkerung Neukaledoniens als kulturelles Erbe zugänglich zu machen und das künstlerische Schaffen zu fördern heißt:

– es den Kanak, alten wie jungen, zu ermöglichen, mit Stolz ihre Wurzeln wiederzufinden;

– den Nicht-Kanak Elemente zu einem gemeinsamen kulturellen Bezugssystem anzubieten, aus dem sich neue Praktiken und eine gemeinsame ozeanische Identität entwickeln können;

– Neukaledonien mitten in einem weltoffenen Netz regionaler Kulturen zu situieren.

Das Kulturzentrum ist die Synthese und das Resultat dieser Zielsetzung.

Die Unterzeichner der Vereinbarungen von Matignon haben diese Geschichte zu schreiben begonnen. Sie waren die ersten, und die, die nach ihnen kamen, haben dieser Münze Perlen hinzugefügt, weiße, schwarze, gelbe – je nach dem Bild der Geschichte, die die verschiedenartigen Menschen dieses Landes noch zu machen haben werden, damit es wirklich das ihre wird.

So haben wir auch, als Herr Staatssekretär Emile Biasini uns am 30. Oktober 1989 mitteilte, daß Herr Premierminister Michel Rocard im Einverständnis mit Präsident Mitterrand beschlossen hat, die Realisierung der A.D.C.K. in die Liste der großen kulturellen Vorhaben der Region aufzunehmen, sofort die Tragweite dieses Projektes begriffen. Wir hatten gleich die Idee, ein Kulturzentrum zu bauen, das uns als geeignetes Werkzeug erschien, um die Aufgaben dieser Organisation zu erfüllen.

Wir haben dieses Kulturzentrum nach einem ganz neuen globalen Konzept geplant: Es sollte das gesamte Feld kultureller Aktion umspannen und Tradition und Moderne der mitten im Wandel begriffenen Kultur der Kanak unter ein und demselben Dach in sich vereinen. Ist das nicht der Weg, den Jean-Marie von Mélanésia 2000 bis zu den Vereinbarungen von Matignon zurückgelegt hat?

Basis des Projekts war für uns der Raum der traditionellen Sitten und Gebräuche, in dem wir uns heute befinden. Er ist das Fundament, das das gesamte Projekt auf der Erde der Kanak legitimiert. Im Herzen des Zentrums wollten wir eine Mediathek, in der man mit Hilfe verschiedener geeigneter Hilfsmittel, wie sie die heutige Technologie zur Verfügung stellt, das Erbe der Kanak-Tradition, ganz besonders der nicht-materiellen Tradition, wiederfinden, sich aneignen und im Kontext der ozeanischen Kulturen insgesamt situieren kann. Schließlich hofften wir hier, ein künstlerisches Schaffen zu ermöglichen, das zeitgenössische Entwicklungen zum Ausdruck bringt und in die Zukunft weist. Für Musik und Tanz, deren Tradition in verschiedener Hinsicht sehr lebendig geblieben ist, und für das weniger entwickelte Theater haben wir uns mehrere Aufführungsräume gewünscht. Der zeitgenössischen Bildenden Kunst ist eine Reihe von großzügigen Räumen vorbehalten, als Werkstatt und als Ausstellungsfläche zugleich. Um diesen Kern herum hat sich das Projekt nach und nach entwickelt.

Ich möchte der französischen Regierung danken, insbesondere allen Kulturministern, die dieses Projekt verfolgt haben, ebenso wie den Ministern für die Überseeprovinzen, die uns mit unerschütterlicher Beständigkeit unterstützt haben. Trotz veränderter Mehrheitsverhältnisse war die Regierung stets für das Projekt da, jede hat ihre Perle hinzugefügt. Sie hat uns immer Vertrauen entgegengebracht, nicht nur, in-

– New Caledonia will be integrated into a regional cultural network that is open to the world

The Cultural Center is a means to fulfil these aims.

The signing parties of the Matignon agreement were the initial authors of the above. They are the currency makers, and others came – and will come – afterwards, adding their own pearls, be they white, black or yellow. History is being – and will be – made by a mix of people who all come from one and the same country.

When Mr. Emile Biasini (the then Secretary of State) announced on 30 October 1989 that the French Prime Minister, Mr. Michel Rocard, had decided with President Mittérand's approval to fund a major center devoted to Kanak culture, we immediately realized just how challenging such a project would be. Straightaway, we thought of building a facility that would serve as a tool for implementing the missions assigned to the A.D.C.K.

The design concept for the Center grew out of one single innovative objective, namely grouping diverse cultural activities in order to bind the traditional and modern aspects of Kanak culture, which is currently in the throes of change. This was precisely the path that was paved by Jean-Marie after Melanesia 2000 up until the Matignon agreement.

We placed the space given over to local traditions and customs at the core of the scheme, which is where we are gathered today. We wanted there to be a multimedia library at the heart of the Center, where people might rediscover and re-appropriate Kanak heritage via varied and adapted supports, rendered accessible by modern technology. More specifically, we sought to relay intangible traditions, by situating them within the context of all South Pacific cultures. And lastly, we wanted to provide the resources for nurturing artistic creation to encourage contemporary expression and to anticipate the future. We envisioned several different performance areas for music, dance, which as traditions have remained wholly alive, as well as for the lesser developed tradition of drama. There is also a series of lofty spaces, dedicated to contemporary artworks. It was thus around this core that the scheme progressively took shape.

I wish to thank the French government, particularly all the ministers of culture who tracked the project, as well as the ministers of overseas territories who provided immeasurable support. Despite the political changes that have occurred, the government has always remained tuned in to the project, each one adding its own pearl. It placed boundless trust in us, not only by giving us a handsome budget of 320 million French francs, but also by allowing us to fully oversee the works, under the remote but effective supervision of the Major Public Works Department, to whom I extend my thanks via Emile Biasini and Jean-Claude Moréno.

Heartfelt thanks also to Michel Rocard, for making the choice he did. I know that many objected to it, saying that such a sum of money could have been spent on something "more useful". However, it is precisely because culture is "not useful" that it forms the very lifeblood of humankind, with dignity being its only price. The aims were to:

dem sie uns ein Budget von 320 Millionen Französischen Francs bewilligte, sondern auch, indem sie uns die Bauherrschaft überließ, die ganz in unserer Verantwortung lag, unter der so effizienten wie weit entfernten Oberaufsicht durch die Mission des Grands Travaux, der ich hier in der Person von Emile Biasini und Jean-Claude Moréno dafür danken möchte.

Besonderen Dank möchte ich Michel Rocard für seine kluge Wahl aussprechen. Ich weiß, daß es viele Einwände gab, mit einer derartigen Summe hätte man andere, «nützlichere» Projekte realisieren können. Doch eben weil sie «nicht nützlich» ist, macht die Kultur das Menschenleben überhaupt aus, und ihr einziger Preis ist dessen Würde. Dieses Projekt als wichtiges Bauvorhaben der Republik einzustufen hieß, sich den Bau eines einzigartigen, herrlichen Schreins vorzunehmen, um dem Volk der Kanak den Stolz auf seine Kultur zurückzugeben. Es hieß auch, diesen Schrein in einer Gegenwärtigkeit, an der niemand vorbeikommt, auf eben der Erde zu errichten, auf der diese Kultur sich herausgebildet hat, um sie der ganzen Welt zu zeigen. Damit wird einem Zustand ein Ende gesetzt, den Jean-Marie beklagte: «Heute kann ich mit einem Nicht-Kanak zwar teilen, was ich an französischer Kultur besitze, aber für ihn ist es unmöglich, mit mir zu teilen, was an meiner eigenen Kultur universell ist.»

Wir haben unser Projekt den Ingenieuren von Beture-Setam erklärt. Ich danke ihnen dafür, daß sie es in klare architektonische Begriffe übersetzt haben, was es uns ermöglichte, einen internationalen Wettbewerb auszuschreiben.

Die Auswahl von zehn großen Architekten durch die zu einem Drittel mit Ozeaniern besetzte Jury hat uns zur Begegnung mit Renzo Piano verholfen. Ich weiß, daß zwischen ihm und Octave Togna der Funke schnell und heftig übergesprungen ist. Das war der Beginn eines schönen Abenteuers. In einem Tag auf dem Gelände hatte Renzo im wesentlichen begriffen, was wir erwarteten, so widersprüchlich es auch erscheinen mochte, die Kultur der Kanak «in die Schachtel» zu packen. So war es denn auch nicht überraschend, daß die Jury sein Projekt auswählte. Kurz darauf stimmte auch der verstorbene Präsident Mitterrand persönlich dieser Entscheidung zu. Darum sei heute sein Andenken geehrt.

Das Werk von Renzo Piano brauche ich Ihnen nicht vorzustellen. Es steht vor Ihnen, an die Halbinsel geschmiegt. Sie können dieses «Symbol der Kanak-Kultur» selbst bewundern, seine «Präsenz», die der Gartenvegetation der Kanak entspringt. Sie können den Wechsel zwischen «niedrigen Strukturen und großen Ausblicken» betrachten, den «sanften, ausgewogenen Übergang von der beständigsten Kanak-Kultur zu den Neuerungsansprüchen der Moderne». Sie können das Spiel von Licht und Schatten mit der Transparenz ahnen. Den Weg hindurch, «bald offen, bald geschützt», doch stets behaglich, werden Sie gleich schätzen lernen. «Erinnerung an die Hütte, die sich auf einen Traum von der Zukunft» öffnet, als rufe unsere Gesellschaft «nach Vollendung». Von dieser Gesellschaft sagte Renzo Piano 1990: «Wenn die Bevölkerung der Kanak sich im Kulturzentrum wiedererkennt, dann werden ihr Mittel zu einem qualifizierten Dialog mit den anderen Gemeinschaften des Landes angeboten.» Aber ich überlasse es Renzo, gleich, wenn wir es besichtigen, selbst über sein Werk zu sprechen.

– Make this project a "major work of the Republic" by designing a unique
  and stunning gem.
– Restore the Kanak people's pride in their culture
– Provide a frame of reference so that this might be conveyed worldwide.

In short, the overall goal was to turn around a situation that Jean-Marie described with regret: "Although I can share with non-Kanaks what I possess of French culture, it is impossible for them to share the universal element of my culture".

We described the project to the structural engineers Beture-Setam, and I wish to express my gratitude to them for having so skillfully translated our thoughts into clear architectural terms, thereby enabling us to launch an international competition. Ten famous architects were selected by the jury (a third of this jury being from the South Pacific) and that is how we met Renzo Piano. Things clicked straight away between him and Octave Togna, marking the start of a wonderful adventure. In just one day spent on the site, Renzo grasped the main thrust of what we wanted, even though we may have appeared rather contradictory, seeking to put Kanak culture into a "box" of sorts. It therefore came as no surprise that Renzo's design was voted winning entry. The scheme was approved by the late President Mitterand shortly afterwards, to whom I wish to pay homage today.

I do not need to describe Renzo's work. It stands there before you, blending with the peninsular. Take time to admire it, this "symbol of Kanak culture" that emerges so forcefully from our Kanak land. Study the alternation between the "low structures and elongated forms", the "gently balanced swing from deep-rooted Kanak culture to the innovative demands of modernity". Look at the hint of shadow and light formed by the play on transparency. See how the path through the Center at times seems open and at others sheltered, yet always intimate. It is "reminiscent of huts opening on to a dream of the future". It is a culmination point for our society, of which Renzo Piano said in 1990: "if the Kanak people can see a reflection of themselves in the Cultural Center, then they will have the means to engage in enriching dialogue with the country's other communities". I will leave it up to Renzo himself to present his work, during our visit of the building later on.

Thank you Renzo for so patiently bearing with us. We were a difficult and demanding client, for we knew we would be managing the building on a daily basis. You were in tune with us throughout all those eight years. We understood one another. The ingenious way in which you have drawn on hi-tech contemporary architecture to reveal the breaks and continuities in Kanak culture, creating a cultural center for the future, has meant that we have not fallen into the trap of becoming self-centered devotees of the past. Instead, we stand squarely among the chorus of other nations. We are so very proud of the international acclaim showered on you. Thank you as well to your loyal team – Paul, William, Dominique, Francis and Sophie from GEC, and all those others who shared the same outlook as us. Alban, I would also like to say a special thank you to you, for your invaluable help.

Ich danke dir, Renzo, daß du diesen Bauherrn ertragen hast, der schwierig und anspruchsvoll war, weil er wußte, daß er im Alltag mit dem Gebäude würde umgehen müssen. In diesen ganzen acht Jahren hast du uns voller Respekt zugehört. Wir haben uns gut verstanden. Das Genie, das du an den Tag gelegt hast, als du die Brüche und die Kontinuitäten der Kanak-Kultur in eine zeitgenössische, hochtechnologische Architektur übersetzt hast, in einen schöpferischen Raum für die Zukunft, hat es uns erspart, in die Falle eines um sich selbst kreisenden Vergangenheitskults zu gehen, und uns auf gleichem Fuß ins Zusammenspiel der Nationen eingereiht. Mit dir zusammen sind wir stolz auf die internationale Anerkennung, die dir zuteil geworden ist.

Ich danke auch deiner treuen Equipe, Paul, William, Dominique, Francis und Sophie vom GEC, und all den anderen, die unsere Sensibilität geteilt haben. Alban, erlaube mir, dich ganz persönlich in diesen Dank einzuschließen, für deinen ganz besonderen Beitrag.

Es war eine schöne Geschichte, dieses Zentrum zu bauen. Es war auch eine schwere Verantwortung, so große Mittel zu verwalten und dabei zu wissen, daß dies in Wirklichkeit erst ein Anfang ist.

Dank an die SECAL, die delegierte Bauleiterin, die uns so gut begleitet hat in allem, worin wir uns nicht auskannten. Ihre Rolle war nicht leicht, zwischen unseren zuweilen zögerlichen Ansprüchen, den legitimen Zielen der Bauherrschaft und überdies dem Druck der Bauunternehmen zu vermitteln. Sie waren immer für uns da, mit gutem Rat, treu in der Rückerstattung, streng und entschieden zugleich.

Es ist auch Ihnen zu verdanken, Jean, Thierry, Ghislain und all den anderen Beratern, die im Schatten gearbeitet haben, daß der Bau, trotz einiger Verspätungen, fertiggestellt worden ist.

Doch hier steht nun das Ergebnis von fünf Jahren der Forschungen und drei Jahren Bauzeit, von Freuden und Zufällen, von Debatten, Abstimmungen und Verhandlungen. Wir haben viel gelernt und viele Höhen und Tiefen erlebt: das Warten auf die Ergebnisse während der Vorversuche; die Spannungen aufgrund des vielfältigen Drucks oder wenn ein Unternehmen absprang; Sorgen wegen des Budgets; die Freude, als die ersten großen Bäume gepflanzt waren; die heftige Bewegung bei der eindrucksvollen Errichtung der ersten Bögen und des ersten Dachs...

Es muß heute ausdrücklich hervorgehoben werden, wieviel dieses Projekt, an dessen Verwirklichung in der Mehrheit örtliche Unternehmen und Arbeiter mitgewirkt haben, zur wirtschaftlichen Dynamik dieses Landes beigetragen hat, nicht nur hinsichtlich der Beschäftigung und der finanziellen Auswirkungen, sondern auch in technologischer Hinsicht. Es ist sehr viel Kompetenz vermittelt worden, und es war ein ständiger Appell, über sich selbst hinauszuwachsen, um wirklich Hervorragendes zu leisten.

Ich danke stellvertretend für alle Unternehmen an dieser Stelle der Firma Glauser International, der die schwere Aufgabe zufiel, Bevollmächtigte der etwa zwanzig Unternehmen zu sein, die direkt beteiligt waren. Sie mögen mir verzeihen, daß ich nicht jedes einzelne nenne, dafür fehlt es an Zeit.

Aber es ist mir wichtig, all die Menschen zu grüßen, die auf der Baustelle gearbeitet haben, Ingenieure und Arbeiter aus aller Herren Länder. Wenn wir über die Baustelle gingen, haben wir sie bei der Arbeit

Building the Center was a beautiful endeavour. It was also a heavy responsibility, given the large amount of resources involved, and knowing that this was just the beginning. Thank you to SECAL, the delegate contracting authority, for having so carefully guided us. Your role was not easy, for you had to deal not only with our requests (which were not always clear-cut), but also with the legitimate objectives of the architects and the pressure of the contractors. You always had your finger on our pulse, giving us the right advice, loyal to the underlying aims of the project, as well as being firm and watchful of every detail. It is also thanks to you – Jean, Thierry, Ghislain and all those consultants who worked in the shadows – that the construction phase was successfully completed, despite a few delays. We can see before us the product of five years of design studies and three years of building works; years that were filled with joy and uncertainty, with dialogue and negotiations. We learnt a lot, and went through some emotional times. There was the anticipation we felt during the preliminary tests; the tension when contractors failed to deliver, leading to pressure and stress; our joy at seeing the first large trees planted; and our intense feelings when our eyes beheld the roof and arches being majestically laid.

It should be noted how much this project – which involved mainly local contractors and workers – has boosted the country's economy, not only in terms of jobs and financial spin-offs, but also in terms of technology. There was a substantial pooling of skills, combined with a constant call to outperform and achieve excellence.

I likewise wish to thank the twenty or so contractors, represented by Glauser International. I hope they will forgive me for not mentioning all of them by name, for I am running out of time.

I would also like to particularly thank everyone who worked on site, including engineers and workers from all walks of life. We used to see them hard at the task, and noted there were a lot of young people. I could see they felt that they were taking part in a great venture, that it was a special moment in their lives. Even though it wasn't always possible to stop and speak with them, I could sense that they loved what they were doing. They are not all here today, but I nonetheless wish to say a special thank you to them. I can see that all our efforts have not been in vain. May the remaining chapters be as eloquent as the ones written so far.

We could not bring you into an empty building, however beautiful it may be, for it is important to show you right from the outset that our culture is very much alive. As of 1990, the Agency began to weave a web of cultural initiatives, which was unusual at the time given that "culture" used to be associated with charity or volunteer work. Initially, there were some people who thought the Center might have been an expensive toy given to the Kanaks to calm the troubled waters. We, however, saw it as a challenge, namely anticipating what shape cultural life might take ten years down the line and responding to this professionally. Here my thoughts are with Marc Coulon, who has recently passed away. I would also like to thank Jean-François Marguerin and Pierre Culand, who helped us maintain quality standards. Thank you as well to Gérauld de Galard and to Bernard Gilman for their unflagging support.

gesehen. Viele junge Leute waren unter ihnen. Ich konnte ihnen anmerken, daß sie sich bewußt waren, ein großes menschliches Abenteuer, einen großen Augenblick ihres Lebens zu erleben. Auch wenn ich nicht oft Gelegenheit hatte, mit ihnen zu sprechen, an ihrer Art, sich in ihre Arbeit hineinzuknien, habe ich gespürt, daß sie es mit Freude taten. Sie sind heute nicht alle hier, aber ich sage ihnen einen besonderen Dank.

Ich sehe, daß all die Anstrengungen nicht vergeblich waren. Mögen die Seiten dieser Geschichte, die noch zu schreiben sein werden, ebenso schön sein wie die, wie wir schon erlebt haben.

Wir wollten vermeiden, daß Sie in ein schönes, aber leeres Gebäude eintreten. Vielmehr sollten Sie schon vom ersten Tag an dort einer lebendigen Kultur begegnen können. So hat die A.D.C.K. ab 1990 begonnen, ein Gewebe kultureller Aktionen zu knüpfen, und dies in einem Land, in dem der Begriff Kultur keine Geschichte hat. Wenn man «Kultur» sagte, dachte man eher an «Kirchweih» oder «Wohltätigkeit». Anfangs glaubten sogar nicht wenige, das Zentrum werde ein hübsches Spielzeug sein, das man den Kanak schenkt, um sie ruhigzustellen.

Es ging also darum, das kulturelle Leben von zehn Jahren vorauszusehen und Vorbereitungen zu treffen, professionelle Antworten zu finden. Ich denke an Marc Coulon, der vor kurzem von uns gegangen ist, und ich danke Jean-François Marguerin und Pierre Culand, die uns geholfen haben, uns immer an der Qualität zu orientieren. Ich danke auch Gérauld de Galard und Bernard Gilman für ihre nie versiegende Hilfe.

Wir haben zunächst die Zusammenarbeit mit kulturellen Vereinigungen und wissenschaftlichen Körperschaften gesucht und dann vor allem in Koproduktionen mit den institutionellen Partnern angefangen, in unserem Land ein neues Bild kultureller Aktionen zu schaffen. Gewiß, die Kulturpolitik ist vielleicht noch nicht ganz auf der Höhe des Ideals, aus dessen Geist sie entstanden ist, aber wir haben ein großes Stück Weg zurückgelegt. Wenn die A.D.C.K. heute ein positives Image hat, so weil wir es zusammen geschaffen haben. Und dies hat nicht wenig zu einer Mentalitätsveränderung beigetragen, zu der sich heute alle beglückwünschen.

Deshalb liegt mir daran, den Präsidenten der Iles-Loyau-té-Provinzen, Nord und Süd, zu danken, ebenso wie ihren Vertretern im Verwaltungsrat und ihren Kultur-Verantwortlichen. Ganz besondere Erwähnung verdient Jean Lèques, der Bürgermeister von Nouméa, denn seine Gemeinde hat uns das acht Hektar große Grundstück gegeben, auf dem wir dieses Kulturzentrum dann bauen konnten. Ich muß auch unsere Zusammenarbeit mit der Equipe des Lacito vom CNRS («Centre National de la Recherche Scientifique», größte Forschungseinrichtung Frankreichs), die heute durch Jean-Claude Rivière hier vertreten ist, sowie die mit der Communauté du Pacifique, vertreten durch M. Robert Dum, erwähnen. Nicht vergessen werden darf ferner die Mitwirkung der Ecole des Hautes Etudes Sociales mit dem Programm ESK, die des Centre Georges Pompidou, das uns drei Bibliothekare geschickt hat, und die der Ecole d'art. Schließlich möchte ich mich für den Rat der Bernheim-Bibliothek bedanken, die vielen Privatper-

We first undertook the task of forging a new cultural image by seeking out partnerships with cultural associations and scientific organizations. We then concentrated on developing joint projects with institutional partners. Although perhaps not all our cultural policies are as noble as their founding ideals, we have nonetheless made a lot of headway. The reason why A.D.C.K. enjoys such a positive image is because we have built it together, resulting in an overall change in attitude that everyone is so pleased with today. That is why I also wish to thank the Presidents of the Northern Province, the Southern Province and of the Loyalty Islands Province, together with their delegates and cultural attachés. Jean Lèques, mayor of Noumea, likewise deserves a special mention since his commune kindly gave us the 8-hectare site on which the Cultural Center now sits.

Mention must also be made of several partnerships. These include the Lacito team of the CNRS [French Science and Engineering Research Council], represented today by Jean-Claude Rivièrre; the Pacific Community, represented by Mr. Robert Dum; the School of Advanced Social Studies and their ESK program; the Georges Pompidou Centre, which assigned three librarians to us; the School of Art; the Bernheim Library; and lastly, all the partnerships formed with private individuals and companies that are too numerous to list here.

During the last three seasons we looked at how the Center could take shape, under the baton of Emmanuel Kasarhérou. Our main concerns were designing the layout, compiling a collection that contained references to contemporary Kanak and South Pacific art, making an inventory of South Pacific cultural players and forming partnerships with them, sounding out the target population, and lastly, setting up and training the team.

Thank you to the representatives of the advisory cultural council that came with us to collect contemporary works from Papua New Guinea and Vanuatu, as well as from the Aborigines in Australia and the Maoris in New Zealand. It was requested that the commissioned works be contemporary but with a traditional slant, so as to display the contemporary output of these communities in a way that reflects ancestral customs.

Thank you to the members of the "Comité de Pilotage". Your support has been crucial, though I will not name you individually as you are part of the family.

Thank you to the members of the Agency's Board of Directors, as well as to those who supported us but who have sadly passed away, including the great chief Luc Bouarate, Séraphin Tiavouane, Auguste Parawi Raybas and Jacques Iékawé.

Lastly, I would like to say a word of encouragement to the team whose job it is to breathe daily life into the Cultural Center. Thank you for all your hard work. You are the successors of the old guard. You are the ambassadors of Kanak culture, and as such you must openly relay it not only to every community in New Caledonia, but to all four corners of the world. The Center's success hinges on you.

As I mentioned at the beginning, this project came to an end just as the Noumea agreement was being

sonen und -vereinigungen nicht mitgerechnet, die ich hier nicht alle nennen kann.

Unter der Leitung von Emmanuel Kasarhérou arbeiten wir nun schon in der vierten Saison daran, das Leben des Zentrums zu planen. Im Mittelpunkt unserer Bemühungen stand, ein szenisches Konzept zu entwerfen und zu installieren, eine Sammlung zusammenzustellen, bei der die zeitgenössische Kunst der Kanak und Ozeaniens maßgeblich sein soll, die kulturellen Akteure im gesamten südpazifischen Raum zu erfassen, mit ihnen Partnerschaften einzugehen, ein Publikum zu schaffen und schließlich die Equipe des Zentrums auszusuchen und auszubilden.

Dank an die Vertreter des Beirats der traditionellen Autoritäten, die uns nach Papua-Neuguinea, nach Vanuatu, nach Australien zu den Aborigenes und nach Neuseeland zu den Maoris begleitet haben, um die zeitgenössischen Ausstellungsstücke in Empfang zu nehmen. Denn diese Werke, so war bei der Bestellung gesagt worden, sollten zugleich zeitgenössisch und traditionell sein, um so hier im Zentrum die Fähigkeiten dieser Gemeinschaften zu einem zeitgenösssischen künstlerischen Schaffen zu repräsentieren, das zugleich die Traditionen der Vorväter achtet.

Vielen Dank auch den Mitgliedern des "Comité de Pilotage". Obwohl ihr Beitrag entscheidend gewesen ist, nenne ich sie nicht einzeln, denn sie gehören zum Haus. Wenn ich den Mitgliedern des Verwaltungsrats danke, möchte ich das Andenken jener ehren, die uns unterstützt haben und die von uns gegangen sind: der große Chef Luc Bouarate, Séraphin Tiavouane, Auguste Parawi Raybas und Jacques Iékawé.

Schließlich will ich die Equipe ermutigen, die das Zentrum alltäglich mit Leben erfüllt, indem ich ihr danke und ihr sage: Ihr seid die Erben der Alten, die an die Kultur der Kanak glaubten; ihr habt die Aufgabe, sie über die Zeit hinwegzutragen. Als Botschafter der Kanak-Kultur müßt ihr sie allen Gemeinschaften des Landes und der ganzen Welt zugänglich machen. Der Erfolg des Zentrums hängt in hohem Maß von euch ab.

Wie ich anfangs schon sagte, wird dieses Projekt in dem Moment fertiggestellt, da die Vereinbarungen von Nouméa unterzeichnet werden. Es fügt sich vollkommen in den Prozeß dieser Vereinbarungen ein, insofern es die Identität der Kanak verstärkt, die der Kern dieser Abmachungen ist. Sie sind das Ergebnis aufmerksamen Zuhörens, des Eingehens auf die Forderungen des Volks der Kanak, in gewisser Weise sind sie der erste offizielle Schritt zum Bau einer gemeinsamen Zukunft.

Ich habe den Eindruck, es ist eine lange Zeitspanne, auf die wir heute zurückblicken. Aber es ist auch klar, daß in zehn Jahren nicht alle Bereiche gleich erfolgreich gemeistert worden sind. Die Wirtschaft hat einen großen Schritt nach vorn gemacht, vor allem in den Großvorhaben. In anderen Bereichen hat es weniger Fortschritte gegeben. Was die Kultur angeht, haben wir das Gefühl, die uns anvertraute Aufgabe erfüllt zu haben. So sollte man diese lange Zeit eher als neue Möglichkeit für die Menschen begreifen, das Werkzeug beherrschen zu lernen, bevor sie die ihnen vom Gesetzgeber übertragenen Kompetenzen ausüben. Es liegt nur an uns zu beweisen, daß man es schaffen will und kann; das wird viel Arbeit von uns verlangen; doch das Resultat liegt in unserer Hand.

signed. This was perfect timing, for the goal that lies at the heart of both the agreement and the Center is to strengthen Kanak identity. The Center is the result of having carefully listened to the demands of the Kanak people. It is, in a way, one of the first official acts of building a common future.

The prescribed time that now stretches before us seems long to me. But it is true that over the last ten years, there are some areas of activity that have not been managed as well as others. For instance, while the economic sector has enjoyed strong growth, other sectors have not been as healthy. As regards the cultural sector, though, it would appear that the mission assigned to us has been successfully completed. We should therefore see this allotted timeframe as an opportunity to learn how to totally master the tools before being given legislative power to fully wield them. It is up to us to show that we can and will succeed. This will require a lot of hard work, but the outcome is in our hands. I urge the Kanaks to commit themselves to this path, especially those who want their independence.

That brings me to the issue of the young people of New Caledonia, who might feel a little distanced today, and yet it was for you that the agreement was signed. You were uppermost in our thoughts when making the choices we did. The Cultural Center can offer you a multitude of events and activities. It will be a place for forging ties between the young people of our country and you must seize this chance, for as Jean-Marie said: "Our identity lies ahead of us".

I truly hope that the Cultural Center will achieve its mission of raising awareness of our culture and cultural values. In our view, art was the best means to fulfil such a task via a purpose-designed building. Now it is a matter of tackling the mystery of humankind. We have to enter people's hearts, listen to them and build together. By playing the role of a melting pot, the Tjibaou Cultural Center can deliver a new message to the West, namely that of respecting others and of respecting national heritage, including nature's flora and fauna. These are the values that distinguish us from others today and which can be shared and perpetuated in the future.

Having witnessed everything since the beginning, we can affirm that Jean-Marie's message has been upheld. And we know that it is now up to us to convey it to future generations and to ensure the Center's success. Thank you to all the cultural bodies who are helping us to spread this new word. I know it is no easy task.

Thank you again to you all, my friends, for coming here today, and in some cases from so far, to share our joy.

Let this be a day of celebration for us all!

Marie-Claude Tjibaou
President of the managing board of the A.D.C.K.

Ich lade die Kanak dazu ein, sich auf diesen Weg einzulassen, ganz besonders natürlich diejenigen, die ihre Unabhängigkeit wollen. Deshalb ein Wort an die Jugend dieses Landes, die sich heute ein wenig ausgeschlossen fühlen mag, obwohl die Vereinbarungen gerade für sie unterzeichnet worden sind. Das Kulturzentrum wird den Jugendlichen des Landes die Möglichkeit zu vielerlei Aktivitäten bieten; es wird für sie ein Ort des Überflusses sein. Sie sollten ohne Zögern diese Gelegenheit ergreifen, die zur Annäherung der verschiedenen Gemeinschaften führen wird, denn, wie Jean-Marie sagte: «Unsere Identität liegt vor uns.»

Ich wünsche mir sehr, daß das Kulturzentrum seinem Auftrag vollkommen gerecht wird. Wir haben uns ein Werkzeug erhofft, das den Menschen ein Gefühl für die Kultur und für Werte gibt, die sie nicht mehr kennen. Wir dachten uns, daß die Kunst der beste Weg ist, um diese Kultur kennenzulernen und daß dieses Gebäude den Zugang erleichtern wird.

Was nun bleibt, ist das Mysterium der Menschen. Man muß zu ihren Herzen vordringen, ihnen zuhören und mit ihnen gemeinsam etwas aufbauen. Wenn das Kulturzentrum J.M. Tjibaou jener Ort der Vermischung wird, von dem eine neue Botschaft an den Okzident ausgehen kann, die der Achtung vor dem Menschen, vor dem anderen, vor dem kulturellen, aber auch dem natürlichen Erbe von Flora und Fauna dient, dann können die Werte, die heute unsere spezifische Eigenart ausmachen, bleibende Werte werden und morgen von vielen geteilt werden.

Wir, die wir von Anfang an dabei gewesen sind, können bezeugen, daß der Botschaft Jean-Maries nicht zuwidergehandelt wurde. Und wir wissen, daß die Weitergabe dieser Botschaft an künftige Generationen und der Erfolg des Zentrums in unserer Hand liegen.

Ich danke den traditionellen Autoritäten, die bei diesem neuen Wort bei uns sind. Ich weiß, daß es für sie nicht einfach ist.

Noch einmal Dank an euch alle, meine Freunde, daß ihr so zahlreich und manchmal von so weither gekommen seid, um unsere Freude mit uns zu teilen.

Möge es heute für uns alle ein schönes Fest werden!

Marie-Claude Tjibaou
Präsidentin des Verwaltungsrates der A.D.C.K.

Discours de Madame Marie-Claude Tjibaou à l'occasion de l'inauguration
du Centre Culturel Tjibaou le 4 mai 1998

Monsieur le Premier ministre,

Madame le Ministre,

Monsieur le Secrétaire d'Etat,

Monsieur le Délégué du Gouvernement,

Mesdames, Messieurs les représentants des gouvernements des pays océaniens,

Monsieur le Sénateur,

Mesdames, Messieurs les Députés,

Monsieur le Président du Congrès,

Messieurs les Présidents des Provinces,

Monsieur le Maire de Nouméa, Messieurs les Maires,

Messieurs les représentants des autorités coutumières,

Messieurs les Présidents du FLNKS et du RPCR,

Chers amis,

Permettez-moi, Monsieur le Premier Ministre, de vous remercier d'avoir répondu si chaleureusement à notre invitation, car, en donnant une dimension nationale au centre culturel Tjibaou, votre présence en signale l'enjeu.

Si nous avons retenu ce jour, bien que le chantier soit à peine terminé, c'est d'abord parce qu'il est l'anniversaire de la mort de Jean-Marie Tjibaou et de Yéiwéné Yéiwéné. Mais l'événement que nous vivons aujourd'hui est beaucoup plus qu'une simple commémoration. En effet, l'achèvement du Centre Culturel coïncide avec la fin de la période des accords de Matignon, et son inauguration se déroule en même temps que se signent les accords de Nouméa qui ouvrent une nouvelle étape dans l'histoire de notre Pays. L'inauguration de ce centre aujourd'hui constitue un signe fort qui incarne l'esprit de Jean-Marie Tjibaou.

Lors des accords de la rue Oudinot, Jean-Marie avait tenu à ce que soit créée l'Agence de Développement de la Culture Kanak pour promouvoir la culture kanak parce que, comme il disait, «nous voulons dire au monde que nous ne sommes pas des rescapés de la préhistoire, encore moins des vestiges archéologiques, mais des hommes de chair et de sang». En donnant à l'Agence la mission d'affirmer la culture kanak dans son patrimoine, mais aussi dans son actualité et ses créations, et en obtenant l'engagement d'avoir un terrain à Nouméa pour y construire cet établissement, il indiquait dès le départ la philosophie qui animerait ce grand projet: inscrire résolument à Nouméa la culture kanak comme référence identitaire de ce pays.

Offrir ainsi le patrimoine kanak en héritage culturel à l'ensemble de la population de la Nouvelle-Calé-

donie et développer la création artistique, c'est permettre aux kanak, anciens et jeunes, de retrouver avec fierté leurs racines, c'est proposer aux non-kanak des éléments de références culturelles communes pour participer à l'émergence de pratiques nouvelles et d'une identité océanienne commune et c'est insérer la Nouvelle-Calédonie au sein d'un réseau culturel régional ouvert au monde.

L'image du centre culturel, c'est la synthèse et la réponse à cette ambition.

Les signataires des accords de Matignon ont commencé à écrire cette histoire. Ces hommes sont la tête de la monnaie, et les autres qui viennent après rajoutent des perles, blanches, noires, jaunes… à l'image de l'histoire qui reste à faire par des hommes différents dans un même pays pour qu'il soit le leur.

Aussi, lorsque, le 30 octobre 1989, monsieur Emile Biasini, secrétaire d'Etat, nous annonça qu'avec l'accord du Président Mittérand, Monsieur Michel Rocard, Premier Ministre, avait pris la décision d'inscrire la réalisation de l'A.D.C.K. sur la liste des grands équipements culturels en région, nous avons aussitôt perçu l'enjeu de ce projet. L'idée s'est immédiatement imposée de construire un centre culturel qui serait l'outil pour la mise en œuvre des missions de l'A.D.C.K.

Ce centre culturel, nous l'avons conçu selon un concept global inédit: il devait, sous la même entité, regrouper l'ensemble du champ d'action culturelle, allier la tradition et la modernité de la culture kanak en pleine mutation. N'est-ce pas le chemin parcouru par Jean-Marie depuis Mélanésia 2000 jusqu'aux accords de Matignon?

88

A la base du projet nous avons placé l'espace coutumier où nous sommes aujourd'hui. Il est le fondement qui légitime l'ensemble sur la terre kanak. Au cœur du centre, nous avons voulu une médiathèque où l'on pourrait retrouver et se réapproprier, à travers des supports variés et adaptés comme le permettent les technologies d'aujourd'hui, le patrimoine de la tradition kanak, et plus spécialement celui de la tradition non matérielle, en le situant dans le contexte de l'ensemble des cultures océaniennes. Enfin, nous avons souhaité nous donner les moyens d'une création artistique pour exprimer les évolutions contemporaines et anticiper l'avenir. Pour la musique et la danse dont la tradition est demeurée, à des titres différents, très vivante, et pour le théâtre, moins développé, nous avons souhaité plusieurs espaces de spectacle. Pour la création et la présentation des arts plastiques contemporains, nous avons réservé une série d'espaces nobles. C'est autour de ce noyau que le projet s'est progressivement développé.

Je voudrais remercier le gouvernement français, et particulièrement tous les ministres de la culture qui ont suivi ce projet, ainsi que les ministres de l'outre-mer qui nous ont apporté un soutien indéfectible. Malgré les changements de majorité politique, le gouvernement est toujours resté à l'écoute du projet, chacun rajoutant sa perle à la monnaie. Il nous a témoigné une confiance constante, non seulement en nous allouant une belle enveloppe budgétaire de 320 millions de francs français, mais aussi en nous laissant gérer la maîtrise d'ouvrage, en toute responsabilité, sous la lointaine et efficace tutelle de la Mission des Grands Travaux que je remercie à travers Emile Biasini et Jean-Claude Moréno.

Je souhaite particulièrement remercier Michel Rocard pour la pertinence de son choix. Je sais que beaucoup ont objecté qu'avec une telle somme, on aurait pu faire aboutir d'autres réalisations «plus utiles». Mais justement, c'est parce qu'elle «n'est pas utile» que la culture est la vie même de l'homme et qu'elle n'a de prix que sa dignité.

– Donner à ce projet le statut de «grand chantier de la république», c'était prendre le pari de construire un écrin unique et superbe,

– pour rendre au Peuple kanak la fierté de sa culture

– et, par sa présence incontournable, l'ériger en référence à cette terre où elle s'est façonnée,

– afin de la présenter au monde entier.

C'était ainsi mettre fin à un regret de Jean-Marie lorsqu'il disait: «Si je peux aujourd'hui partager avec un non-kanak ce que je possède de culture française, il lui est impossible de partager avec moi la part d'universel contenue dans ma culture».

Ce projet, nous l'avons expliqué aux ingénieurs du Beture-Setam. Je les remercie d'avoir bien su le traduire en termes architecturaux clairs qui nous ont permis de lancer un concours international.

La sélection de dix grands architectes, par un jury, composé pour un tiers d'océaniens, nous fit rencontrer Renzo Piano. Je sais qu'entre lui et Octave Togna, le courant passa vite et fort. Ce n'était que le début d'une belle aventure. En une journée sur le site, Renzo avait saisi l'essentiel de ce que nous attendions, malgré tout ce que cela pouvait avoir de contradictoire de mettre la culture kanak «en boîte». Aussi, ce ne fut pas une surprise, lorsque le Jury choisit son projet. Peu après, le défunt Président Mitterand approuvait lui-même ce choix. Sa mémoire en est aujourd'hui honorée.

Je n'ai pas besoin de vous présenter l'œuvre de Renzo. Elle est devant vous, épousant la presqu'île. Vous pouvez admirer ce «symbole de la culture kanak», «présence» émergeant de la végétation horticole kanak. Vous pouvez contempler l'alternance des «structures basses et des grandes échappées», la «transition douce et équilibrée entre la culture kanak la plus pérenne et les exigences novatrices de la modernité». Vous pouvez deviner les ombres et les lumières jouant de la transparence. Vous pourrez en apprécier «le parcours, tantôt ouvert, tantôt abrité» mais toujours intime. «Souvenir de Case, ouvert sur un rêve d'avenir», comme un «appel à l'achèvement» de notre société dont Renzo Piano disait en 1990, «si la population kanak se reconnaît dans le centre culturel, alors lui seront offerts les moyens d'un dialogue de qualité avec les autres communautés du pays». Je laisse à Renzo le soin de parler lui-même de son œuvre, tout à l'heure, lorsque nous la visiterons.

Merci Renzo de ta patience à supporter ce maître d'ouvrage compliqué et exigeant puisqu'il savait qu'il aurait à gérer le bâtiment au quotidien. Tu as su nous écouter avec respect tout au long de ces huit années. Nous nous sommes bien compris. Le génie que tu as manifesté en traduisant dans une architecture contemporaine et de haute technologie les ruptures et les continuités de la culture kanak, espace de création pour demain, nous a évité de tomber dans le piège du passéisme autocentré et nous introduit

de plain-pied dans le concert des nations. Nous sommes fiers avec toi de la reconnaissance internationale qui vient de t'être décernée.

Merci aussi à ta fidèle équipe Paul, William, Dominique, Francis et Sophie du GEC et tous les autres qui ont partagé avec nous la même sensibilité. Alban, permets-moi de t'associer personnellement à ces remerciements, pour la contribution singulière que tu as su y apporter.

Ce fut une belle histoire que de construire ce centre. Ce fut aussi une lourde responsabilité que de gérer de si gros moyens, en sachant que ce n'est, en fait, qu'un début.

Merci à la SECAL, maître d'ouvrage délégué, d'avoir su si bien nous accompagner dans ce qui n'était pas notre métier. Votre rôle n'était pas facile, entre nos exigences parfois hésitantes et les légitimes ambitions de la maîtrise d'œuvre, puis la pression des entreprises. Vous aussi avez su être à l'écoute, de bon conseil, fidèles dans la restitution, rigoureux et fermes à la fois.

C'est grâce à vous aussi, Jean, Thierry, Ghislain, et tous les consultants qui ont travaillé dans l'ombre, que le chantier a bien abouti, malgré quelques retards.

Mais voilà le résultat de cinq années d'études et de trois années de chantier, de joies et d'aléas, de discussions, de concertations et de négociations. Nous avons beaucoup appris et nous avons eu beaucoup d'émotions: l'expectative des résultats lors des essais préalables; la tension des défections d'entreprises et celle des pressions multiples; les inquiétudes budgétaires; la joie des premiers grands arbres plantés; l'intense émotion de l'impressionnante pose des premiers arcs et de la première toiture...

Il convient de souligner aujourd'hui combien ce projet, en associant dans sa réalisation une majorité d'entreprises et de travailleurs locaux, a contribué à la dynamique économique du pays, non seulement en terme d'emploi et de retombées monétaires, mais aussi en terme de technologies. Il y a eu de nombreux transferts de compétences, et un constant appel à se surpasser pour présenter l'excellence.

Je remercie les entreprises à travers la société Glauser International qui avait la lourde tâche d'être le mandataire de la vingtaine d'entreprises qui sont intervenues en direct. Qu'elles m'excusent de ne pas toutes les citer, car je manque de temps.

Mais je tiens à saluer les gens qui ont travaillé sur le chantier, ingénieurs et ouvriers de toutes origines. Quand nous passions sur le chantier, nous pouvions voir leur travail. Il y avait beaucoup de jeunes gens. J'ai bien perçu qu'ils sentaient qu'ils vivaient une grande aventure humaine, un grand moment de leur vie. Même si je n'ai pas eu souvent la possibilité de parler avec eux, à la manière dont ils se sont impliqués dans leur travail, j'ai senti qu'ils aimaient ce qu'ils faisaient. Ils ne sont pas tous ici aujourd'hui, mais je leur dis un merci particulier.

Je vois que tous les efforts engagés n'ont pas été vains. Puissent les pages à inscrire être aussi belles que ce que nous avons déjà vécu.

Nous ne pouvions pas vous faire entrer dans un beau bâtiment vide. Il fallait que vous puissiez, dès aujourd'hui, y rencontrer une culture bien vivante. Dès 1990, l'Agence a commencé à nouer les fils d'un tis-

su d'action culturelle dans un pays où ce concept n'avait pas d'histoire. Lorsqu'on disait «culture», on pensait alors plutôt «kermesse» et «bénévolat». Ils n'étaient pas rares, au départ, ceux qui pensaient que le centre serait un beau joujou donné aux kanak pour calmer le jeu.

Or l'enjeu était d'anticiper ce que pourrait devenir la vie culturelle dix ans plus tard et de se préparer à y répondre avec professionnalisme. Je pense à Marc Coulon qui nous a récemment quittés, et je remercie Jean-François Marguerin et Pierre Culand qui nous ont aidé à tenir le cap de la qualité. Merci également à Gérauld de Galard et à Bernard Gilman pour leur soutien sans faille.

C'est d'abord dans la recherche de partenariats avec les associations culturelles et les organismes scientifiques, puis surtout à travers les coproductions conduites avec les partenaires institutionnels, que nous avons entrepris de construire progressivement une nouvelle image de l'action culturelle dans ce pays. Certes, les politiques culturelles ne sont peut-être pas encore toutes à la hauteur de l'idéal qui en a inspiré le lancement, mais nous avons fait beaucoup de chemin. Si aujourd'hui l'A.D.C.K. bénéficie d'une image positive, c'est parce que nous l'avons construite ensemble. Et cela n'a pas peu contribué à un changement des mentalités dont tout le monde se félicite aujourd'hui.

C'est pourquoi je tiens à remercier les Présidents des Provinces Iles Loyauté, Nord et Sud, ainsi que leurs représentants au conseil d'administration et les responsables de leurs affaires culturelles. Une mention toute spéciale à Jean Lèques, le maire de Nouméa, puisque sa commune nous a donné le terrain de 8 hectares sur lequel nous avons pu construire ce centre culturel. Il faut aussi mentionner nos partenariats avec l'équipe du Lacito du CNRS, représentée aujourd'hui par Jean-Claude Rivière; celle de la Communauté du Pacifique représentée par M. Robert Dum; la coopération de l'Ecole des Hautes Etudes Sociales avec le programme ESK; celle du Centre Georges Pompidou qui nous a délégué trois bibliothécaires, et celle de l'Ecole d'art ; le conseil de la Bibliothèque Bernheim; sans compter les nombreux partenariats avec des personnes et sociétés privées que je ne peux pas toutes nommer ici.

Depuis trois saisons, nous avons commencé à préfigurer la vie du centre, sous la conduite d'Emmanuel Kasarhérou. Concevoir la scénographie et la mettre en place, constituer une collection qui fasse référence à l'art contemporain kanak et océanien, recenser les acteurs culturels de l'ensemble du Pacifique Sud, nouer avec eux des relations de partenariat, créer un public, constituer et entraîner l'équipe, ont été au centre de nos préoccupations.

Merci aux représentants du conseil consultatif coutumier qui nous ont accompagnés en Papouasie-Nouvelle-Guinée, à Vanuatu, en Australie chez les Aborigènes et en Nouvelle-Zélande chez les Maoris pour réceptionner les œuvres contemporaines monumentales. En effet, celles-ci avaient été commandées dans des conditions à la fois contemporaines et coutumières, de manière à représenter dans ce centre la capacité de création artistique contemporaine de ces communautés, dans le respect de leurs traditions ancestrales.

Merci aux membres du Comité International de Pilotage du Projet culturel. Bien que leur apport ait été

déterminant, je ne les nommerai pas individuellement, parce qu'ils font parti de la maison. En remerciant les membres du conseil d'administration, je voudrais saluer la mémoire de ceux qui nous ont soutenus et qui nous ont quittés: le grand chef Luc Bouarate, Séraphin Tiavouane, Auguste Parawi Raybas et Jacques Iékawé.

Enfin, j'encouragerai l'équipe qui fait vivre le centre culturel au quotidien en la remerciant et en lui disant: vous êtes les héritiers des vieux qui ont cru en la culture kanak; vous êtes chargés de la projeter dans le temps. Ambassadeurs de la culture kanak, vous devez la présenter ouverte à toutes les communautés du pays et au monde entier. Le succès du centre dépend beaucoup de vous.

Comme je le disais en commençant, ce projet aboutit alors que l'on signe les accords de Nouméa. Il s'inscrit parfaitement dans le processus des accords de Nouméa dans la mesure où il vient renforcer l'identité kanak qui est au cœur du dispositif. Résultat de l'écoute attentive des revendications du Peuple kanak, il est, en quelque sorte, l'un des premiers actes officiels de la construction d'un avenir commun. En jetant un coup d'oeil en arrière, j'ai le sentiment que le délai qui s'ouvre aujourd'hui devant nous est long. Mais on se rend compte que sur dix ans, tous les secteurs n'ont pas été maîtrisés avec le même bonheur. Le secteur économique a fait l'objet d'une forte avancée, surtout dans les grands projets. D'autres secteurs ont moins bien progressé. Pour le secteur culturel, nous avons le sentiment d'avoir tenue la mission qui nous était confiée. Donc il convient de prendre ce délai comme une nouvelle possibilité offerte aux gens pour maîtriser l'outil avant d'exercer pleinement les compétences prévues par le dispositif législatif. Il ne tient qu'à nous de démontrer qu'on peut et qu'on veut réussir; ça nous demandera beaucoup de travail; mais le résultat dépend de nous.

J'invite les kanak à s'engager dans cette voie, et notamment ceux qui veulent leur indépendance. Et cela me conduit à dire un mot pour la jeunesse de ce pays qui peut se sentir un peu exclue aujourd'hui, alors que l'accord a été signé pour les jeunes. Je tiens à lui dire combien elle est présente dans nos choix. Le centre culturel lui offrira de nombreuses propositions d'activité; il sera un lieu de foisonnement pour la jeunesse de ce pays. Qu'elle n'hésite pas à l'investir pour se saisir de cette opportunité qui contribuera au rapprochement des communautés, car, comme le disait Jean-Marie, «notre identité, elle est devant nous».

Je forme tous mes vœux pour que le centre culturel accomplisse au mieux sa mission. Nous avons souhaité un outil qui remplisse sa fonction de sensibilisation à la culture et à des valeurs que les gens ne connaissent pas.

Nous avons pensé
– que l'art est une voie d'introduction privilégiée à la connaissance de cette culture;
– que le bâtiment en faciliterait l'accès.

Maintenant, il reste le mystère des hommes. Il faut entrer dans leur cœur, les écouter et construire ensemble. Si donc le centre culturel Tjibaou devient ce lieu de brassage, d'où peut partir un message nou-

veau vers l'occident, celui du respect de l'homme, de l'autre, du patrimoine culturel et aussi naturel de la flore et de la faune, alors les valeurs qui font aujourd'hui notre spécificité pourront demain être partagées et pérennisées.

Nous qui avons été là depuis le début, nous pouvons affirmer qu'il n'y a pas eu transgression du message de Jean-Marie. Et nous savons que sa transmission aux générations futures et la réussite du centre sont maintenant entre nos mains.

Merci aux autorités coutumières qui nous accompagnent dans cette parole nouvelle. Je sais qu'elle n'est pas simple pour eux.

Merci encore à vous tous, mes amis, d'être venus si nombreux, et parfois de si loin, pour partager notre joie.

Qu'aujourd'hui soit une belle fête pour nous tous!

Marie-Claude Tjibaou
Présidente du conseil d'administration de l'A.D.C.K.

Der Alltag im Centre Culturel Tjibaou

Hin und wieder gibt es Bauwerke, deren Zauber die Einweihung nicht überdauert, weil die Ideen, die zu ihrer Planung und Verwirklichung geführt haben, im Alltag schnell vergessen werden. Das Kulturzentrum gehört sicherlich nicht zu ihnen.

Auch drei Jahre nach seiner Einweihung übt das Centre Culturel Tjibaou auf seine Besucher unfehlbar einen Zauber aus, der sie zutiefst berührt. Das sagen mir alle einheimischen und ausländischen Besucher, die ich Gelegenheit hatte und habe herumzuführen. Mehr noch, die meisten derer, die wie ich das seltene Privileg haben, tagtäglich dort zu arbeiten, empfinden die Harmonie zwischen der von Renzo Piano geschaffenen Architektur und der Funktion dieses Orts sehr stark.

Eine Architektur für ein Zentrum der Kanak-Kultur

Über die gewöhnlichen Fragen hinaus, die sich einem Architekten bei der Konstruktion eines derartigen Gebäudes stellen, war hier die deutliche Beziehung zu bedenken, die das Projekt zur Kultur der Kanak haben sollte. Die Schwierigkeit für den Architekten bestand darin, einen Weg zu finden zwischen der Versuchung des Anekdotischen, das zur allzu getreuen, d.h. servilen Reproduktion traditioneller Formen führt, und dem Willen, sich von diesen Formen zu emanzipieren und eine zu radikal innovatorische Lösung vorzuschlagen. Das eine wie das andere ist hier vermieden worden, es wurde eine eigenständige Lösung gefunden, eine Mischung aus der «Erinnerung an die Hütte», wie Renzo Piano es formuliert, und seiner eigenen Schöpfung. Und diese subtile Alchemie ist es, die den Besucher bei jeder Annäherung an das Gebäude ergreift.

Die Einfügung der Architektur in die Landschaft

Der Grundgedanke des Architekten, daß sich das Gebäude der Landschaft anpassen, sogar anschmiegen sollte, drückt sich in den offenen, schlanken Formen der Hütten und in der besonderen Positionierung der Konstruktion aus. Das Hauptgebäude, ein runder, kaum abgestützter Bogen, zu den Passatwinden hin errichtet, unterstreicht die subtile Spannung zwischen einer windzugewandten und einer windabgewandten Seite, zwischen einer Seite, die sich der Bewegung und dem Handeln, und der anderen Seite, die sich der Stille und Reflexion öffnet, wie es Renzo Piano am Anfang in seinem Wettbewerbsentwurf formuliert hat. Diese Eigenheit der Landschaft wird von der Architektur also nicht nur nicht beeinträchtigt, sondern sogar verstärkt. Das Gebäude stellt sich dem Wind nicht entgegen, sondern schmiegt sich ihm an, vereint sich mit ihm und schenkt so dem Besucher eine natürliche Luftbewegung und das Gefühl von Harmonie.

The Centre Culturel Tjibaou in Everyday Life

There are some buildings that lose their magic after being opened to the public, with everyday use eroding the initial design concept. The Tjibaou Cultural Center is certainly not such a building. Inaugurated three years ago, it inexorably continues to cast a magic spell. Everyone I have shown around – whether they be local or from abroad – has confirmed this. And those of us who, like myself, have the untold privilege of working in the Center on a daily basis, keenly feel the harmony between Renzo Piano's design and the building's function.

An Architectural Design for a Kanak Cultural Center

Other than the usual challenges that face an architect when constructing this type of building, there was also the question of how to make the design scheme a celebration of Kanak culture. The main worry was not to stray into the realm of folkloric imitation, yet at the same time not to be too radically modern. Renzo Piano's response was to propose a highly original design with shell-like buildings resembling traditional Kanak huts. It is this subtle alchemy, bearing Piano's hallmark, that strikes visitors the moment they approach the building.

Blending the Building into the Site

The architect's underpinning concept was that the Center should merge with its surroundings, by drawing on the site's resources. In other words, he sought to marry the building to its natural setting, which he achieved via two strategies: first by the way he positioned the building, and second, by designing the huts as open, slender forms. The main building – a hovering, crescent shaped structure – sits facing the trade winds and is characterized by a subtle tense pull between the side that fronts the wind and the side that is turned away from it, i.e. between the side that reaches out to active movement and the other that seeks peace and a thought-inspiring setting. This was the design formula Renzo Piano presented during the competition phase. It is a formula that does not place the building and site in opposition to one another, but rather welds them together to create a sensation of transparency, natural ventilation and harmonious relations.

The transparent effect of the building is just as much physical as it is visual. It can be felt at each step, as the sea breezes brush against one's body, and is intensified at certain times of the day and seasons of the year by the play of light that is so particular to the Pacific. It is partly due to this physical sensation – created by natural ventilation and the building's integration with is site – that the Center seems to blend into its surroundings. In fact, it seems to have grown with the site rather than having landed there. From the

Die «Transparenz», die der Architekt so liebt, ist nicht nur visuell. Sie ist eine physische Wirklichkeit, die man durch die Luftzirkulation vom Meer her auf Schritt und Tritt körperlich erfährt. Noch erweitert durch das je nach Tages- und Jahreszeit wechselnde, für den Pazifik so typische Spiel des Lichts, trägt sie stark zu dem Eindruck bei, daß Gebäude und Landschaft ein Ganzes bilden, nicht nur topographisch, sondern auch klimatisch.

So in seine Umgebung eingefügt, scheint das Gebäude eher gewachsen als dort hingestellt worden zu sein. Schon zu Beginn seiner Arbeit hatte Renzo Piano gesagt, die Kultur der Kanak drücke sich für ihn nicht in einer zeitüberdauernden, ostentativen Architektur aus, sondern eher in einer «Kunst der Landschaft», für die er uns hier ein Beispiel liefert.

Der Kanak-Weg und Mwakaa

Für den Kanak, der das Zentrum besucht, rechtfertigen zwei Räume die ihm sich darbietende zeitgenössische Architektur: der «Kanak-Weg» und der den traditionellen Gebräuchen gewidmete Raum «Mwakaa». Der eine wie der andere sind ebenso eng mit der Kultur der Kanak verbunden wie mit der Architektur. Sie sind von der A.D.C.K. geplant und entwickelt worden, und mit dem Architekten wurde ihr Zusammenhang mit der architektonischen Konzeption durchgesprochen.

Der traditionelle Raum, «Mwakaa» genannt, was soviel heißt wie «Häuptlingssitz», «Ort der Versammlung zu den zeremoniellen Festen», war von Anfang an für diesen Zweck vorgesehen und ist beim Wettbewerb den Architekten nicht unterbreitet worden. Dieser Raum sollte ein Ort der Erinnerung sein, der die althergebrachten Räume evoziert, ohne sie indessen auf eine möglichst identische Reproduktion zu reduzieren. So situiert sich der «Mwakaa»-Raum symbolisch in der Tradition der Kanak, doch er transponiert sie in eine neue Form, die Elemente verschiedener regionaler Traditionen in sich vereinigt. Dieser Ort der Erinnerung ist auch als Ort des Lebens gedacht. Die Hütten dienen der Unterbringung von Gästen, und nicht selten entdecken die Besucher des Zentrums überrascht, daß die Hütten gelegentlich bewohnt sind...

Der «Kanak-Weg» führt auf der Nordseite des Hauptgebäudes durch fünf Landschaftsgärten und ermöglicht dem Besucher einen Spaziergang durch Raum und Zeit. Er basiert auf dem Mythos von Téâ Kanaké, einer mythischen Gestalt aus dem Land paicî-cèmuhî, Namensgeber des Kanak-Volkes und Einiger unserer Kultur insgesamt. Wir haben nicht von ungefähr auf diesen Mythos und diese Gestalt zurückgegriffen. Ihr Name evoziert den Begriff «kanak», den sich unser Volk vor fast zwanzig Jahren für sich selbst ausgewählt hat. Außerdem hat ihn, wohl aus denselben Gründen, schon Jean-Marie Tjibaou in dem Theaterstück verwendet, das er 1975 für das Festival Mélanésia 2000 schrieb. Dies hat uns dazu ermutigt, weiter daran zu arbeiten, die alten symbolischen Elemente in neue Kontexte zu stellen. Der «Kanak-

very outset Piano stressed how he envisioned Kanak culture as being expressed through a type of "landscape art" rather than through showy, monumental architecture.

Tracing the Kanak Path and Mwakaa

For Kanak visitors, there are two spaces that legitimize the architectural scheme. These are the "Kanak Path" and the "Mwakaa" space dedicated to local traditions and customs. Both areas are intimately connected with Kanak art and architecture and were designed by the Agency for the Development of Kanak Culture. However, Renzo Piano was consulted, to ensure overall coherence.

"Mwakaa " means "chieftanship". It is a place for holding ceremonial events, and this is thus the role allocated to the Mwakaa space in the Cultural Center, though the program was not presented to the architects during the competition phase. It is invested with memories of the past and hints at tradition, symbolically featuring Kanak customs in a new way. In addition, it was designed to be lived in, with the huts serving as accommodations. Visitors to the Center are quite often surprised to see that these huts are actually occupied.

The "Kanak Path" runs along the north side of the main building. It is a string of five landscaped gardens offering visitors a stroll in time. The ensemble is based on the myth of Tea Kanake, founding mythical ancestor of the Paici-Cemuhi land and Kanak people, and thus acts as a federating element for the whole Cultural Center. It is clearly not by chance that the legend of Tea Kanake was selected, for the name contains the word "Kanak", chosen almost twenty years ago by the Kanak people to refer to themselves. In fact, Jean-Marie Tjibaou used it even before that (undoubtedly for the same reasons) in the description of the staging for the Melanesia 2000 festival in 1975. We simply decided to further develop this approach of incorporating old symbolic elements into new contexts. The "Kanak Path" is an open-air exhibition area based on plant life. The aim was not to promote botany as such, but rather to evoke Kanak culture, by postulating that whatever the visitor's culture or origins, their senses will be stirred when seeing the site's protected plants and natural surroundings. This was a totally logical approach, given that our culture is primarily expressed through the works of nature. In addition, the idea of using a path and a story line to reach out to people's awareness seemed much closer to our traditional means of communicating knowledge. The architect is to be applauded for having grasped the importance of plant life and contextual features, and for having entrusted us with this part of the project.

Weg» ist ein museales Angebot unter freiem Himmel, bei dem die Lebewesen, was Pflanzen ja sind, nicht zu einer bloß botanischen Begegnung einladen sollen, sondern das in die Kultur der Kanak einzuführen versucht, denn jeder Mensch, gleich welcher Kultur, nahmen wir an, würde empfänglich sein für die Pflanzen und die besonders geschützte Natur an diesem Ort. Da sich unsere Kultur vor allem durch Gegenstände der Natur ausdrückt, ist es ganz natürlich, daß wir darauf zurückgegriffen haben. Außerdem schien uns der Gedanke, sich Wissen auf dem Weg einer Wanderung und einer Geschichte zu erwerben, sehr viel näher an unseren traditionellen Arten der Wissensvermittlung. Es gereicht dem Architekten sehr zur Ehre, daß er die Bedeutung der Pflanzen und der Umwelt begriffen und uns diesen Teil des Projektes anvertraut hat.

Räume und Funktionen

Die Planung und der Bau des Centre Culturel Tjibaou haben sich über einen Zeitraum von acht Jahren hingezogen, in dessen Verlauf sich das architektonische in Übereinstimmung mit dem kulturellen Projekt weiterentwickelte. Zu den Funktionen der Räume hat es verschiedene Vorschläge gegeben, bevor der aktuelle Stand festgelegt wurde. Das kulturelle Projekt gliedert sich in drei große Funktionsbereiche: der erste ist die Präsentation von Tanz-, Musik- und Theater-Aufführungen, der zweite die Präsentation von Werken der Bildenden Kunst, und der dritte dient der Lektüre und dokumentarischen Forschungen. Die Untergliederung in diese Funktionsbereiche drückt sich architektonisch in verschieden dimensionierten, mal innen, mal außen liegenden Räumen aus, die es erlauben, die Umsetzung dieser Funktionen je nach Bedarf zu modifizieren. Was die Aufführungen angeht, verfügen wir über ein gedecktes Theater mit 400 Plätzen und zwei Freilicht-Theater mit 1000 und 2500 Plätzen. In der Praxis benutzen wir meist das gedeckte und das größere der beiden Freilicht-Theater. Zeitweilig werden für kleinere Aufführungen auch andere Räume in oder außerhalb des Gebäudes umgerüstet. Für die Bildenden Künste ermöglichen es uns Ausstellungsräume unterschiedlicher Größe, mit einer Gesamtfläche von 1100 m², sowohl Großveranstaltungen wie die «Biennale für zeitgenössische Kunst Nouméa», die die gesamte Fläche in Anspruch nimmt, als auch kleinere Ausstellungen aufzunehmen. In der Praxis verwenden wir oft auch andere Räume des Zentrums für Ausstellungen, etwa die 200 Meter lange Zentralallee oder die Gärten draußen. Diese Art der Präsentation im Freien erwies sich als besonders geeignet für bestimmte Formen der pazifischen Kunst. Die Mediathek schließlich ist in drei Hütten untergebracht und verfügt über eine erstklassige elektronische Ausstattung, die dem Benutzer vor Ort eine außerordentlich reiche Grundlage bietet, über seine Mauern hinauszustrahlen und sich in das Netz der Dokumentations- und Forschungszentren für die Pazifik-Kulturen einzuklinken. Die Frage, ob sich Räume und Funktionen im Lauf der Entwicklung wirklich als zueinander passend erweisen, stellt sich häufig bei dieser Art von Ausstattung. Un-

Dedicated Areas and Functions

The design of the Tjibaou Center and its ensuing construction stretched over a period of eight years, during which the architectural scheme and cultural program evolved in tandem. Diverse proposals were put forward for the roles of each area before the final choice was made that visitors can see today. It was decided to have three major spaces: one for performance art, another for artworks and one for reading and documentary research. These key functions have been allotted specific spaces (interior and exterior) with varied proportions that can be altered in line with needs. For instance, we have a covered theater that can seat 400 people and two outdoor theaters with a seating capacity of 1,000 and 2,500. In practice, we tend to mainly use the covered theater and 2,500-seat outdoor space. For smaller shows there are other interior and exterior spaces that can be fitted out on a temporary basis. The exhibition areas all have completely different surface areas but they can be put together, totalling around 1,100m^2. This enables us to host both small-scale exhibitions and signal events such as the "Contemporary Art Biennial of Noumea", during which we use the whole display area. We can also temporarily convert other spaces in the Center into exhibition space, such as the outdoor gardens or 250m-long pathway. This procedure of displaying works outside is particularly suited to certain forms of Pacific art. Lastly, there is the multimedia library, which takes up three huts accommodating the last word in IT equipment. Not only does the library provide users with a wealth of information on site, it is also a vehicle for hooking up to the worldwide network of documentary resource centers devoted to Pacific cultures. There is, nonetheless, one nagging question, which is how can the library keep pace with its function? However, the past three years have revealed that the initial design has stayed in tune with developments and should continue to do so.

The Cultural Center is the flagship component of a project that is designed to raise awareness of Kanak culture and to forge ties with other cultures in New Caledonia. It exudes life, reflecting the country's many cultural facets and diverse communities, which barely twenty years ago had no real common denominator. Now, these selfsame communities have a place for meeting and sharing cultural experiences. They have a Center that is more than a regional pole of artistic creation; it is a genuine hub that sits at the crossroads of international cultural exchange.

In sum, the Tjibaou Cultural Center is much more than just a building. It is one whole in which the masterly creativeness of an architect has been merged with the past, present and future of Kanak culture, highlighting how culture is a dynamic process that is constantly changing and on the move.

Emmanuel Kasarhérou
Cultural Director of the A.D.C.K. / Tjibaou Cultural Center

sere jetzt dreijährige Erfahrung zeigt, daß die ursprünglichen Lösungen nicht grundsätzlich in Frage gestellt werden mußten und wohl noch lange Bestand haben werden.

Das Centre Culturel Tjibaou ist Teil eines Gesellschaftsprojekts, das vor allem auf der Anerkennung der Kanak-Kultur und ihrer Begegnung mit den anderen Kulturen Neukaledoniens aufbaut. Es ist ein lebendiger Ort, der sein kulturelles Angebot im Einklang mit den kulturellen Aktivitäten eines Landes entwickelt, in dem solche Aktivitäten noch vor zwanzig Jahren auf ihren einfachsten Ausdruck reduziert waren und die Gemeinschaften, aus denen es sich zusammensetzt, sich nur schwer eine gemeinsame Zukunft vorstellen konnten. Heute bietet das Zentrum den Bewohnern dieses Landes einen Raum für kulturelle Begegnungen und Auseinandersetzungen, es ist auch ein Anziehungspunkt des regionalen künstlerischen Schaffens, und es situiert sich selbst als Ort des internationalen Austauschs zwischen den Kulturen.

Weit mehr als ein simples Gebäude, ist das Centre Culturel Tjibaou ein Ganzes, in dem sich der schöpferische Schwung eines zeitgenössischen Architekten mit der Achtung vor der tausendjährigen Kultur der Kanak verbindet und die Dynamik eines in ständiger Bewegung begriffenen kulturellen Prozesses ihren Ausdruck findet.

100 Emmanuel Kasarhérou
Kultureller Leiter der A.D.C.K. / Centre Culturel Tjibaou

Le Centre Culturel Tjibaou au quotidien

Il est parfois des bâtiments dont la magie ne survit pas à leur inauguration car le quotidien de leur existence fait vite oublier les idées qui ont présidé à leur conception et à leur réalisation. Le Centre Culturel Tjibaou n'est certes pas de ceux-là.

Trois ans après son inauguration le Centre Culturel Tjibaou produit immanquablement sur ses visiteurs une magie qui les émeut. Tous les visiteurs locaux ou internationaux à qui j'ai eu l'occasion de faire visiter ce lieu me le disent. Bien plus, la plupart de ceux qui comme moi ont le privilège rare d'y travailler au quotidien ressentent fortement l'harmonie de l'architecture de Renzo Piano et de la fonction du lieu.

Une Architecture pour un Centre Culturel Kanak

Outre les habituelles interrogations qui se posent à un architecte pour la construction d'un bâtiment de ce type, s'est posée ici celle de la relation forte que le projet devait entretenir avec la culture kanak. La difficulté consistait pour l'architecte à se frayer un passage difficile entre, d'une part, la tentation de l'anecdotique, qui conduit à une reproduction trop fidèle voire servile de formes traditionnelles, et d'autre part la volonté de s'en émanciper en proposant une solution trop radicalement novatrice. L'une comme l'autre ont été ici évitées, au profit d'une proposition originale posée entre «souvenir de case» ainsi que le formule Renzo Piano et une création qui lui est propre. C'est cette alchimie subtile que le visiteur saisit dès son approche.

L'Integration de l'architecture au site

L'idée fondamentale de l'architecte que le bâtiment devait s'intégrer au site, le respecter en utilisant ses ressources, en un mot l'épouser, trouve sa traduction dans les formes ouvertes et élancées des cases et dans le positionnement particulier qu'il a donné à sa construction. Le bâtiment principal en arc de cercle à peine soutenu, posé face aux vents alizés, marque une tension subtile entre une face au vent et une face sous le vent, entre une face tournée vers le mouvement et l'action et l'autre vers la quiétude et la réflexion, ainsi que l'avait initialement formulé Renzo Piano lors du concours architectural. Cette caractéristique du site, loin d'être contrariée par l'architecture, s'en retrouve ainsi affermie. Sans s'opposer au vent, le bâtiment l'épouse et se conjugue à lui pour offrir au visiteur une ventilation naturelle et un sentiment d'harmonie.

La «transparence» du bâtiment chère à l'architecte n'est pas seulement visuelle. Elle est une réalité physique que l'on peut saisir à chaque pas de la visite par la circulation de l'air venu de la mer. Elle est amplifiée selon les heures et les saisons par le jeu des lumières si propres au Pacifique, et contribue forte-

ment au sentiment que le bâtiment fait corps avec le site, non seulement en sa topographie mais aussi en sa situation climatique.

Fortement intégré au lieu, le bâtiment paraît avoir poussé plutôt que d'y avoir été posé. Renzo Piano avait formulé dès le départ de son travail, que pour lui, la culture kanak ne s'exprimait pas par une architecture permanente et ostentatoire, mais plutôt par un «art du paysage» dont il offre ici une transposition.

Le Chemin Kanak et Mwakaa

Pour le visiteur kanak deux espaces légitiment la proposition architecturale contemporaine: il s'agit du «Chemin kanak» et l'espace coutumier «Mwakaa». L'un comme l'autre de ces espaces sont étroitement liés à l'expression de la culture kanak et à l'architecture. Ils ont été conçus par l'Agence de Développement de la Culture Kanak et leur cohérence avec le projet architectural a été discutée avec l'architecte. L'espace coutumier appelé «Mwakaa » qui signifie «la chefferie», «le lieu du rassemblement des fêtes cérémonielles», est un espace qui dès le départ avait été réservé pour cet usage et n'avait pas été soumis aux architectes lors du concours. Cet espace se devait d'être un espace de mémoire, qui évoque les espaces coutumiers traditionnels sans pour autant les réduire à une reproduction à l'identique. Aussi l'espace «Mwakaa» prend son assise symbolique dans la tradition kanak, mais il la transpose en une proposition nouvelle où s'assemblent des éléments traditionnels régionaux. Ce lieu d'évocation a été aussi pensé comme un lieu de vie. Les cases servent d'hébergement, et il n'est pas rare que les visiteurs du centre soient surpris de découvrir que ces cases ont parfois des habitants…

Longeant la face nord du bâtiment principal, le «Chemin kanak» est un cheminement en cinq jardins paysagés qui propose au visiteur une promenade dans le temps et l'espace. Basé sur le mythe du Téâ Kanaké, personnage mythique du pays paicî-cèmuhî, celui-ci incarne l'ancêtre éponyme du peuple kanak et sert ainsi de fédérateur à notre ensemble culturel. Le recours à cette mythologie et à ce personnage n'est pas fortuit. Son nom évoque le terme «kanak» choisi depuis près de vingt ans par le peuple kanak pour se désigner. Il avait d'ailleurs déjà été utilisé, sans doute pour les mêmes raisons, par Jean-Marie Tjibaou dans l'écriture du jeu scénique du festival Mélanésia 2000 en 1975. Ceci nous a encouragé à poursuivre notre travail d'utilisation d'éléments symboliques anciens dans des contextes nouveaux. Ce «Chemin kanak» est une proposition muséographique à ciel ouvert, utilisant les êtres vivants que sont les plantes, non pas pour inviter à une simple rencontre botanique, mais pour tenter d'introduire à la culture kanak, en postulant que tout humain, quelle que soit sa culture d'origine, serait sensible aux plantes et à l'environnement particulièrement protégé du site. Notre culture s'exprimant principalement par les objets de la nature, c'est tout naturellement que nous y avons recouru. Par ailleurs, l'idée d'un chemine-

ment et d'une histoire pour accéder à une connaissance nous paraissait beaucoup plus proche de nos modes traditionnels de transmission de connaissance. C'est tout à l'honneur de l'architecte d'avoir saisi l'importance de l'environnement et de la plante et de nous avoir confié cette partie du projet.

Espaces et fonctions

La conception et la réalisation du Centre Tjibaou se sont étendues sur une période de huit années, au cours de laquelle le projet architectural et le projet culturel ont évolué de concert. Les fonctions des espaces ont connu diverses propositions avant d'être fixées en l'état actuel. Trois grandes fonctionnalités structurent le projet culturel du Centre Tjibaou: une fonction de représentation de spectacles vivants, une fonction de présentation d'œuvres plastiques et une fonction de lecture et de recherche documentaire. Ces principales fonctions trouvent leur traduction spatiale en des espaces spécifiques de dimensions variées, tant intérieurs qu'extérieurs, permettant de moduler les mises en œuvre en fonction des besoins. Dans le cas du spectacle vivant nous disposons d'un théâtre couvert de 400 sièges et deux théâtres de verdure de 1000 et 2500 places. La pratique nous conduit à utiliser principalement le théâtre couvert et l'espace extérieur de 2500 places. Pour des spectacles plus modestes d'autres espaces intérieurs ou extérieurs du centre sont équipés temporairement. Pour les arts plastiques des espaces d'exposition de surface différentes totalisant près de 1100 m², permettent l'accueil d'événements phares comme la «Biennale d'Art Contemporain de Nouméa» qui utilise la totalité des surfaces, ou d'expositions au format plus réduit. La pratique nous conduit à utiliser temporairement d'autres espaces du centre comme lieu d'exposition, comme par exemple l'allée centrale, longue de 250 mètres, ou les jardins extérieurs. Ce mode de présentation en extérieur s'avère particulièrement adapté à certaines formes d'art du Pacifique. Enfin, la médiathèque occupe trois cases et dispose en outre d'un équipement informatique de pointe lui permettant d'offrir sur place à l'usager un fond d'une grande richesse et de rayonner au delà de ses murs pour s'insérer dans le réseau des centres de ressources documentaires pour les cultures du Pacifique. L'évolution de l'adéquation entre les espaces et les fonctions est une interrogation récurrente pour ce type d'équipement. L'expérience acquise depuis trois ans montre que les propositions initiales n'ont pas été fondamentalement remises en cause et qu'elles ne devraient pas l'être avant longtemps.

Le Centre Culturel est partie prenante d'un projet de société bâti notamment sur la reconnaissance de la culture kanak et sur sa rencontre avec les autres cultures présentes en Nouvelle-Calédonie. C'est un lieu vivant qui développe son offre culturelle en résonance avec l'activité culturelle d'un pays où, il y a seulement vingt ans, elle était réduite à sa plus simple expression et où les communautés qui le composent n'envisageaient qu'avec difficulté un avenir commun. Il offre aujourd'hui aux habitants un espace de

rencontres et de confrontations culturelles, il est aussi un pôle régional de création artistique et se situe au carrefour des échanges culturels internationaux.

Bien plus qu'une simple construction, le Centre Culturel Tjibaou est un tout, qui concilie l'élan créateur d'un architecte de notre temps et le respect d'une culture kanak millénaire, pour traduire la dynamique d'un processus culturel en perpétuel mouvement.

Emmanuel Kasarhérou,
Directeur Culturel de l'A.D.C.K. / Centre Culturel Tjibaou

1991–1998
Tjibaou Cultural Center
Nouméa, New Caledonia

Client: Agence pour le Développement de la Culture Kanak

Renzo Piano Building Workshop, architects Genova – P. Vincent, senior partner in charge

Competition, 1991
Design team: A. Bensa (ethnologist); Desvigne & Dalnoky (landscaping); Ove Arup & Partners (structure and ventilation); GEC Ingénierie (cost control); Peutz & Associés (acoustics), Scène (scenography)

Preliminary Design, 1992
Design team: A. Chaaya, D. Rat (architects in charge) with J. B. Mothes A. H. Téménidès and R. Phelan, C. Catino, A. Gallissian, R. Baumgarten; P. Darmer (models)

Consultants: A. Bensa (ethnologist); GEC Ingénierie (cost control); Ove Arup & Partners (structural & MEP engineering concept); CSTB (environmental studies); Agibat MIT (structure); Scène (scenography); Peutz & Associés (acoustics); Qualiconsult (security); Végétude (Planting)

Design Development and Construction phase, 1993–1998
Design team: D. Rat, W. Vassal (architects in charge) with A. El Jerari, A. Gallissian, M. Henry, C. Jakkman, P. Keyser, D. Mirallie, G. Modolo, J. B. Mothes, F. Pagliani, M. Pimmel, S. Purnama, A. H. Téménidès and J. P. Allain (models)

Consultants: A. Bensa (ethnologist); Agibat MIT (structure); GEC Ingénierie (MEP engineering and cost control); CSTB (environmental studies); Scène (scenography); Peutz & Associés (acoustics); Qualiconsult (security); Végétude (planting); Intégral R. Baur (signing)

Werner Blaser:

Mies van der Rohe – Farnsworth House
Weekend House / Wochenendhaus
ISBN: 3-7643-6089-5 deutsch / englisch

Mies van der Rohe – Lake Shore Drive Apartments
High-Rise Building / Wohnhochhaus
ISBN: 3-7643-6090-9 deutsch / englisch

Mies van der Rohe – Crown Hall
Illinois Institute of Technology, Chicago
The Department of Architecture / Architektur Fakultät
ISBN: 3-7643-6447-5 deutsch / englisch

Tadao Ando – Architektur der Stille / Architecture of Silence
Naoshima Contemporary Art Museum
ISBN: 3-7643-6448-3 deutsch / englisch

Begegnungen / An Architect meets Architects
ISBN: 3-7643-6314-2 deutsch / englisch

Birkhäuser – Publishers for Architecture
P.O. Box 133, CH-4010 Basel, Switzerland.
www.birkhauser.ch